CROSSING OVER

A MEMOIR

LIFE AFTER A NEAR-DEATH EXPERIENCE

Sue Halvorsen

EAGLE ROCK PUBLISHING

Crossing Over is a work of nonfiction.
Some names and identifying details
have been changed to protect the privacy of the individuals.

Published in the United States by Eagle Rock Publishing, LLC,
2350 W Highway 89A #1019, Sedona, Arizona

Cover photo by Tabatha Hines. Copyright © 2022 Tabatha Hines
Book Design by Sandy Cathcart, Needle Rock Press

Identifiers: Library of Congress Control Number: 2018906586 |

ISBN 9781732425101 | ISBN 9781732425118 (ebook)

HALVORSEN, SUE, Author

CROSSING OVER
SUE HALVORSEN

I dedicate this book to God

my best friend and comforter.

Contents

Chapter 1

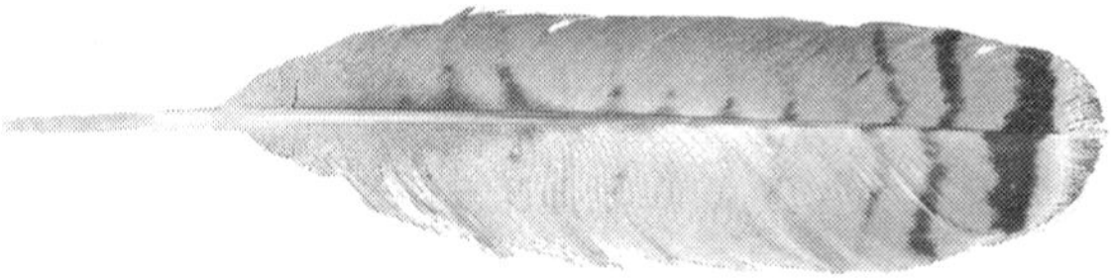

The Whisper

South Bend, Indiana, 1975

I LEAN OVER THE COFFIN, "Grandma it's me," I whisper. "I'm here now."

Grandma doesn't answer me.

She is dressed in a light blue formal gown, and her white hair is spread around her. She looks like an angel.

I hear a man's voice, and I look up. He points at me, but he is not talking to me. He's speaking with a lady I don't know dressed in black. "This is Sue," he tells her, "Mary's oldest granddaughter. She's twelve years old."

A long line stretches behind me, people waiting their turn to see Grandma, but I am not ready to leave her side. They can move around me and still see her.

Grandpa comes up and puts a hand on my shoulder. "You meant the world to her," he says. "The last thing she wrote is in that birthday card you're holding."

I look down at my hands. My birthday card sparkles with angels flying in the clouds. I wonder if Grandma is now flying with those angels.

I don't need to open the card to know what she wrote, "To the best granddaughter this side of heaven. Love, Grandma."

I had received the card a couple of weeks ago when Grandma was in the hospital. I was sure she was going to get better and come home. It hadn't occurred to me she was using my birthday card to say goodbye.

The Catholic church we attended had not prepared me for this moment. Traditions and rules had never given me a God who would be of any comfort. I decide religion is dead, and God doesn't care about me.

So, where does that leave Grandma? Where is she? And is there any kind of life after death?

I feel pain in the pit of my stomach. Grandma will never be coming home.

Grandpa moves away, and my mother takes his place. "Are you all right?"

"Yes," I say. But I'm not. Nothing is all right.

Mom moves away, and a steady stream of people place their hands on my shoulder and tell me how much I meant to my grandma.

I'm numb to their words. I wish they would all leave and let me be alone. Grandma is an angel now, and if they will all leave, I think she may be able to talk to me. Her Eastern Star pin shimmers in the dim light. I take in every detail. I've never seen her wear anything other than gardening clothes and capris. Today, she is dressed in a puffy blue formal just like the angels sitting atop Christmas trees.

Finally, all the people move away, but a strange man comes up and asks me to take a seat in the front row. I do as he says and sit on the edge of my seat, staring at Grandma, but the curtain begins to close. We all wait in anticipation. For what? I don't know.

Then the black curtains part, and I gasp.

The lid is closed. Grandma is inside that closed black box with a line of men in black suits standing next to her.

I can't breathe. Surely, they won't leave her in that box. The loss overwhelms me, and I almost pass out.

When we walk to the grave, I feel like a zombie. Everything is a blur on the ride home.

"Are you okay?" my mother keeps asking.

"Yes," I say, but we both know it's not true.

As soon as the car stops in the driveway, I jump out and run as fast as possible through row after row of field corn. Somewhere in the middle of the field, I fall to the ground and let the pain I had stuffed inside me come to the surface. It shoots out like a geyser, and I scream at the top of my lungs.

“Nooo!” I yell again and again. The pain of losing my best friend is too much.

I stay there for hours and wail until nothing is left but my shattered heart.

Chapter 2

The Light

Mitchell, South Dakota, 1988

"EVERYTHING IS GOING TO BE ALRIGHT," the doctor said as the anesthetic began its work.

But instead of going unconscious, I floated up and out of my body toward the operating lights. The pain I had been experiencing for months was suddenly gone.

I continued to rise like a helium balloon—past the lights, through the ceiling, above the earth, and into a dark universe filled with stars. I had never felt so free.

One star shone more brilliant than the others, drawing me straight to its center. It loomed larger and brighter as I neared. When I reached for the light, liquid love entered my body and flowed through my veins, filling my entire being and cleansing every cell. I basked in the feeling of rightness for a moment. I was perfect. Then, I leaped for the center of all that brightness.

Immediately, a hand grabbed my ankle, stopping me from entering the light.

Suspended in space and time, I stared at the golden brilliance emanating from the star. An amazing source of oneness and love radiated from inside. I was a part of all that oneness and love. I was one with everything, and the oneness was perfection. Yet, amazingly, I was still an individual. I was still me. At the same time, I knew the answer to every question I ever wanted to ask. I knew *everything.*

Again, I tried to leap into the light, but the grip on my ankle tightened. I could go nowhere.

"Sue, Sue, Sue," a voice called, while the hand pulled me back.

I struggled to resist, stretching for the light.

The hand tightened even more.

"Sue, Sue, Sue." The voice grew louder.

"No!" I yelled. "I want to stay!" But as hard as I struggled, the light grew smaller as the grip pulled me away. Wispy gray clouds formed and swirled around me like a tornado. The grip pulled me down a tunnel that soon completely surrounded me.

I clawed at the walls of mist, but the hand pulling me was too strong. I gained incredible speed as I fell through the vortex. Then, I heard a high-pitched whistle, and the circular wall of clouds began to look like streaks of blue and gray. I traveled unbelievably fast until I slammed back into my physical body.

It was as if a lightning bolt had hit the ground.

Being back in my body felt confining and tight, like suffering in a pair of pants that were too small. I opened my eyes halfway and saw a face hovering over me.

“Sue,” said nurse Jenny. “It’s time to wake up. Your exploratory surgery is over.”

What?

Where had I just been? What was that incredible place? And why was I not able to stay?

My vision blurred, and my eyelids grew heavy. Violent shivers wracked my body as I drifted back into unconsciousness.

I had come so close.

Chapter 3

Signs of Hope

HOURS LATER, DR. ELIZABETH STOOD BESIDE ME, staring at my chart. An entire troop of interns formed a half circle at the foot of my bed. Scott, my husband, sat in a chair next to me, weeping.

"You have stage three or four cancer," Dr. Elizabeth said, "and it has spread throughout your body."

All air left my lungs, and my body stiffened. I was only twenty-four years old. Stage four cancer is the worst, and that was what the doctors found in my grandma during her surgery. Three weeks later, she died.

I looked for signs of hope from the others, but everyone stared at the floor, except Scott. His hands covered his face as he wept. The room was full of people, but no one said a word, and the only sound was the inconsolable weeping from Scott.

But then, I heard a buzz. It sounded like a photocopier scanning an image. At the same time, an electrical sensation started at the top of my head and ran down my body, as if I was going through some kind of transforming scanner. No one else in the room showed signs they could hear the buzz, and no one else seemed aware anything was happening.

The sensation continued down my body in healing waves until it exited my feet. Every bit of fear left my body.

I smiled at Dr. Elizabeth and shouted, "I'm healed!"

She flinched, then she patted my shoulder. Her reaction was one of pity. Her expression showed she thought I was in denial of the bad news she had just given me.

I understood her concern, but nothing could shake the surety I had been healed. No one else in the room had felt what I had felt, no one else had seen the amazing things I had seen, and no one else had traveled to that incredible place where I had been.

Still, I agreed to meet with an oncologist for the surgery Dr. Elizabeth was sure I needed. In truth, I was hoping to return to that amazing place I had visited in my near-death experience. Another surgery might take me back there.

Chapter 4

No Fear

SCOTT WAS IN SHOCK. We had been married for less than two years, and now he was told he might lose his wife to cancer.

We remained silent on the drive to our townhome in Yankton, South Dakota. Neither of us knew what to say. We had to process what had just happened.

Before I met Scott, I worked for a CPA full time while attending school to become an accountant. Accounting was not the thing I wanted to do, but my parents had convinced me it would be a great job. What I really wanted, my big dream, was to save animals and teach people about the value animals can bring to one's soul. I melted in tears every time I saw a wounded animal, and I loved the outdoors.

I should have stuck with the dream. Even though accounting was a great career and a guaranteed job, sitting behind a desk and computer all day in an office filled with black and gray filing cabinets drove me nuts. I paced my office like a caged animal.

One day, I wrote "I QUIT" on a bright yellow note and left it on my boss' desk. Afterward, I drove to my college and dropped all my courses even though I was just months from earning my degree. Then…I went fishing.

My parents were shocked, but I felt free. I was back in nature.

A week later, I found a job driving for a pizza franchise. I hoped it would give me plenty of time to enjoy the outdoors. I was quickly promoted to the management team and moved up the corporate ladder.

That's when I met Scott. He was my supervisor and boss. We hit it off and started dating. After the second date we already knew our dreams lined up, and we wanted the same things in life. Ours was the perfect romance story. Three weeks later in July, he asked me to marry him. With Scott's sister's encouragement, at Thanksgiving break, we eloped during a family ski vacation.

Before long, we were the proud owners of a pizza franchise. We had worked hard in Indiana and Chicago to earn the privilege to franchise in South Dakota. We were just getting ready to open our second store in Yankton.

Now, it seemed none of that mattered. This cancer detour was not in our plans.

Even though I wasn't worried about the cancer, because I knew I had been healed, the near-death experience had changed everything for me. I had visited a realm I had never known existed, a realm where everything was perfect. How could I go back to my old way of life and pretend nothing had happened?

After I was released from the hospital, Scott and I headed to our pizza franchise where he told our employees the news. He left our manager in charge.

Early the next morning, Scott and I drove from our home in Yankton to Sioux Falls, South Dakota, to meet the oncologist. I was still sore from yesterday's exploratory surgery, but we began walking up the seven flights of stairs to his office. Our footsteps echoed across the steel and concrete stairwell as we passed each floor. Holding onto the smooth rail, I finally made it to the top.

Three people sat in the waiting room where Scott and I joined them. One middle-aged woman was crying. An older man and woman waited patiently, showing no emotion. I scanned the wallpaper, a subtle pink and gray flower pattern, when a photo of a twelve-year-old boy dressed in traditional middle eastern attire caught my eye. The name beneath revealed he was the doctor's son.

There were no windows, so I stared at the picture of the boy, wondering what my doctor would be like. I started to sweat as the middle-aged woman continued to cry. My attention shifted to her. Was she facing some horrible news she didn't know how to deal with?

The nurse called my name. Scott squeezed my hand as I rose to follow her. The examination room had no windows. I felt caged and alone. I changed into a pink gown and sat on the end of the exam table staring at the walls. The exam room was sterile and cold, and I wished I were outside. I've always loved the outdoors, where everything is vibrant.

When Doctor Semir entered, he asked if I was scared.

"I don't know. Should I be?"

"Most patients are," he said. "I will be your oncologist and surgeon. I saw the pictures of the tumors from your exploratory surgery, but don't worry. I've never lost a patient yet, and you're not going to be the first."

His kind dark eyes looked straight into mine. His voice, softly soothing, comforted me. Although it had been twenty-four hours since I received the bad news, I was still confident I would be fine, but the unknown is never comfortable.

When Dr. Semir finished the exam, the nurse led me to a private conference room where Scott waited. When Dr. Semir joined us, I asked him why no one else had discovered the tumors. "After all the visits to emergency rooms, doctors, and specialists," I said, "you would think someone would have discovered them before now. Why didn't they?"

He shook his head. "They are hard to detect and usually only found in later stages." He sat down at the table, pulled out a diagram of the organs of the human body, and explained what he and the medical team would be doing.

I stared at the diagram and tried to focus on his words, but he suddenly stopped talking.

I looked up to discover his kind eyes filled with sadness. He took a deep breath and said, "I'm sorry, but you are never going to be able to have children."

I looked at Scott and smiled.

He smiled back.

"Thank goodness," I said.

Dr. Semir fell back in his chair and stared at me, speechless. He finally spoke. "That's not the reaction I expected."

"My mother worked nights and slept days, so I spent my childhood taking care of my five siblings. I also had to babysit the neighbor's kids because I was experienced. Every step of the way was an adventure I never really wanted to live. Those were the days of cloth diapers, and every time I think of kids, I think of when my little brother was playing in the pig trough, and I actually had to clean worms from his diaper. I've never wanted any children of my own since."

"I've always been good with that," Scott said. "I just want my wife to be fine."

Dr. Semir shook his head. "I spent the last few hours trying to figure out how to tell you this. Most women are devastated."

He used his chart to show us how the goal was to remove as many organs and tumors as possible to save my life, but he wouldn't know for sure until he looked inside. "Are you okay with signing a paper saying I can do what I deem best once I can see the full story?"

Scott was wringing his hands as I signed the paper. I wasn't nervous at all. It was as if I was in a protective bubble. I just knew I had been healed and would be fine.

Dr. Semir took the paper. "This surgery needs to take place as soon as possible."

I didn't tell the doctor I believed I was healed, because I didn't want another reaction like Dr. Elizabeth's, but I felt absolutely no fear as we left his office. Scott and I had one night together before I would undergo major surgery.

Chapter 5

I Knew

CHECKING INTO THE HOSPITAL the following day, I felt excited because I knew I had been healed. More than anything, I wanted to return to the shining star I had visited during my exploratory surgery when the doctors discovered cancer.

Two orderlies came in and moved me to a gurney. Scott followed me down the hall and, while in the elevator, one of the orderlies asked, "Is there anything we can get for you?"

"A candy bar," I said. I hadn't eaten in days.

Everyone laughed.

I was going to be fine. I just knew it, but I couldn't explain why or how to anyone else. I had only one thought. I wanted to explore the place I was forced to leave during the first surgery. I was not afraid this time, because I knew what to expect.

Or, at least, I thought I did.

Once inside the operating room, I met some of the surgery team. Then off to sleep I went for the second time that week. The surgery took seven hours. For me, it felt like one second. That was it. There were no visions and no new worlds to explore. The disappointment was overwhelming.

I was getting ready to beg for the morphine the doctor promised.

Dr. Semir grabbed my arm. "Sue," he said. "It is a miracle! A miracle!"

I tried to focus, but my vision was too blurred.

"It's a miracle!" He said again. "You're going to be all right."

I could barely see him, but I recognized his voice. His news didn't surprise me. But the excruciating pain I felt in my body was another story.

Dr. Semir explained that he had found none of the expected tumors they had seen in the exploratory surgery. They were all gone!

He did, however, discover a large tumor on one of my ovaries and another on my uterus. So, instead of the expected removal of multiple organs, he ended up only doing a hysterectomy and removing my appendix and stomach fat.

My stomach looked like Frankenstein's forehead. For three days, I couldn't walk because all my stomach muscles were cut vertically and held together with staples. The nurse made me stand several times a day, which was progress enough. A full recovery would take three months.

I spent the next few days staring out the window, wishing I were outside in nature, smelling the fragrant spring air instead of disinfectants in the hospital. I could find no rest in that place. I begged Dr. Semir to tell the nurses to leave me alone so I could sleep. He released me three days later, exclaiming that he had never seen someone recover so quickly.

The moment the nurse wheeled me out of the hospital, my spiritual senses came alive. They were close to the level of heightened awareness I had during the near-death experience. I was mesmerized. Ordinary flowers, grass, and trees seemed more vibrant, more colorful, more full of life. They swayed with the breeze in a rhythm I had never seen before. A rhythm that seemed as old as the earth.

Once in the car, all I could do was stare out the window. As we passed fields of grain, I watched as wheat swayed in the breeze. The stalks seemed to be waving at me. They flowed with order and rhythm, and the patterns reminded me of a well-orchestrated dance performance. They danced in patterns of waves that spoke to my soul. Every hue and tone surpassed anything I had ever witnessed. It was like seeing into another world.

"Look at those wheat fields," I said.

Scott turned and peered out the window and then back at me. "What am I looking for?"

"Wow! That's amazing," I said as we passed a cornfield.

"Where?" Scott tried to look while driving.

"The cornstalks and wheat. They're dancing," I said. "And they're in perfect rhythm."

Scott just shook his head.

When we arrived home, I stared at the houseplants. They were alive in a way I had never experienced before. It was as if I was looking at them with different eyes, eyes that saw in a different realm—a spiritual realm.

"Scott, do you see this?"

"See what?"

"The plant. Do you see it?"

"I see the spider plant. Why?"

"This is so amazing!" I pointed. "It's moving."

Scott stared at the plant and then at me. His entire face was a question mark. Clearly, he didn't see what I saw.

Sitting at the dinner table, I told Scott about my experience during the first surgery. I hadn't told anyone yet, because I didn't want people to think I was crazy. I was convinced the place I had visited during my exploratory surgery had something to do with how I was now seeing things.

Scott agreed.

We needed answers. Why was I seeing things differently, and what exactly happened during the exploratory surgery?

We decided to start with the doctor at my next appointment, which was two weeks away.

Chapter 6

Torture

A WEEK AFTER MY SURGERY, things began to change. Every time I drifted to sleep, regardless if for a nap or for the night, I went to hell. The nightmare was always the same. I was floating on my back at the top of a vortex, which sucked me down. I struggled to wake and stop the descent, but nothing worked. The descent wasn't fast, but it remained consistent with a humming noise coming from the vortex walls until I hit bottom. The stone slab beneath me felt like ice.

I was utterly alone and helpless.

Each time I tried to move, my arms and legs remained stuck to the slab. I would look up and see lightning bolts flashing inside the tunnel's gray walls. Terror gripped me every time, and I struggled to free myself, while the smell of burning and rotting flesh drifted over me in waves.

I was in a pit somewhere beneath the earth.

Dark brown pus oozed from the walls, forming puddles on the stone floor. Flickers of light illuminated some of the connecting tunnels. I could hear cries, wails, and moans along with the clanging of chains on what sounded like prison cell bars. Ugly and grotesque creatures walked by, but none spoke to me. They didn't even acknowledge my presence.

A hammer pounded on metal somewhere in the distance, and people screamed as if they were being tortured. I wanted to scream and run, but I couldn't move or make a sound. The oppressive air was stale like a hot, muggy day.

I didn't belong here, but how could I get out?

Finally, when I thought I would lose my mind completely, the sound of the vortex opening above me hummed like a small jet engine. The tunnel would open up, and I would begin to rise while still sprawled on my back.

I felt utterly helpless, suspended in air with white mist swirling around me. I desperately wanted to wake and escape. I screamed the whole way back, not knowing if I would make it to the surface. When I finally did reach the top, I would hear a loud, sharp smack as if someone had clapped their hands hard next to my ear.

Every time I woke, I was covered in sweat and gasping for air. This was my life every time I fell asleep for an entire week. I begged Scott not to let me fall asleep again, but it was no use.

Then, on the seventh night, the nightmares abruptly stopped. I was rising out of hell through the tunnel when lightning flashed from what appeared to be closed blinds. They were big flashes of light I had never seen before. When I reached the top of the vortex and opened my eyes, everything was quiet. The flashes of light were gone, and I was never taken back to hell again.

The two extremes, first the near-death experience, then hell, left me wondering about the spiritual realm. Yes, I wanted to return to that beautiful place of light I had experienced in the hospital. But the horrible pit beneath the earth seemed just as real. I certainly didn't want to end up there.

It's one thing when you hear people talk about hell, it's another to have experienced it. I had never thought about hell as a real place. My only background in religion came from Sunday school teachers when I was a kid. I remember pictures of a red devil with a pitchfork, nothing like what I had seen in my dreams. None of what I learned in Sunday school had ever seemed real. Now, I began to wonder. *What was real and what wasn't?*

I shared my thoughts with Scott.

"You need to call and set an appointment with the doctor," he said. He meant well, but he had no idea how to fix me.

I thought about my options. Should I go to a doctor, or should I go to a church to find out what happens to you when you die?

Suddenly, I was brought back to a time when I was ten years old sitting in a Roman Catholic church. I had risen to my feet and followed my sister to the altar for Communion. When I moved closer to the priest, who was handing out the Sacraments, I turned and looked at my mother. She was sitting alone in the pew we had just left. She was not allowed to join us as punishment for divorcing my father.

Everyone knew why my mother sat there alone while the rest of us made our way to the altar. She felt humiliated, guilty, and ashamed, an embarrassment in front of others.

Anger rose in me, not at my mother, but at the priests.

How cruel. How dare they do this to her!

She left my father because he was abusing us. The church wouldn't forgive her or grant an annulment, even though the priests had the facts. The church showed no mercy, grace, or forgiveness. She was being punished, because she saved us from a life of hell.

In my ten-year-old mind, the priests and nuns were the abusers. They were the ones trying to kill me by leaving me with an abusive father. I wanted to run out of there and never come back. But that was not an option; I was only a child. So, I did the only thing I could. I refused to listen or believe anything they said. I would not obey anyone who was that cruel. I soon became numb to anything they said. I paid no attention to my Sunday school teachers and would do the opposite of what they asked. I rebelled against anything religious.

Now, at twenty-four, I still wanted nothing to do with the church, so I called the doctor to set up an appointment. Perhaps he would be able to explain what happens when we die.

Chapter 7

The Question

DR. SEMIR WAS PLEASED to see how well my healing had progressed.

"How can I help you?"

"What happens after you die?"

"Why do you ask?"

"I'm curious." I was afraid to tell him what had happened during the first surgery and also about the hellish nightmares I experienced the first week at home.

"Why so curious?" he asked again.

"I really need to know."

Concerned, Dr. Semir took Scott into another room. Scott told me later that Dr. Semir asked him what had been going on, so Scott told the doctor everything I'd gone through the last two weeks. Dr. Semir listened intently, then made a call to a colleague.

When he and Scott returned to my room, he recommended I see a psychiatrist.

I had never seen a psychiatrist before. "What will he do?"

"He will be able to answer your question. He can see you right now, and he's just next door."

I could hardly contain myself as we entered the waiting room. It wasn't long before the nurse called my name.

The psychiatrist was sitting behind a desk when I walked into his office. A big man with glasses and gray hair, he appeared very scholarly. "Your surgeon has already filled me in on the details," he said. "However, I have a few questions."

He then proceeded to ask meaningless questions about my family and friends.

Finally, I grew impatient and interrupted. "What happens to you when you die?"

He looked down at something on his desk while I waited on the edge of my chair. "Now Sue," he said, "let's not rush into anything." He looked up at me. "I want you to come back tomorrow and take a test."

"A test?"

"Don't worry." He smiled. "It's not hard."

I sat there with my mouth open. *How hard was it to answer a simple question? How could a test get me any nearer to the answer?*

He explained he would see me the following day, as he nearly pushed me out the door.

The next day, I arrived early. The strange test was filled with similar questions worded in different ways, as if someone was trying to trick me into answering differently each time. I saw no way it would help me in finding the answer I sought. When I finished, I handed the packet to the doctor and returned to the waiting room.

A half hour later, he called me into his office. He was looking at my results.

"What was the test for?" I asked.

He set the test aside. "I had to see if you were mentally stable."

Seriously? I wondered what on earth I had gotten myself into. Were these people going to throw me into the loony bin? "Well," I said, "Did I pass?"

He finally looked up at me. "Yes."

"So now, can you tell me what happens when you die?"

He suddenly became very talkative, avoiding my question and asking more of his own. It seemed he didn't believe the test results, and he sure didn't know the answer to my question.

I left the office more frustrated than before. "He's a fake," I told Scott. "I'm never going back."

I had another appointment with Dr. Semir, so I told him how I felt. "That psychiatrist you sent me to will not answer my question."

"Why not?"

"I don't know," I said, "but I'm not going back."

He recommended another psychologist, Dr. Michaels, promising this one would be better.

I decided to give him a try.

Dr. Michaels was easier to talk to and intent on trying to help.

I liked him. I was careful about how I asked my questions, because I was afraid he might think I was crazy. But on the next visit, I planned on easing into the question that seemed to freak out the other doctors.

A week later, I skipped up to the office for my next appointment. The door was locked. Posted on the door was a legal notice stating that the medical license of Dr. Michaels had been revoked due to a malpractice allegation.

I stared at the sign. Could this really be happening?

When I saw Dr. Semir at my next follow-up appointment, he had heard the news about the doctor he had recommended. He told me Dr. Michaels had lost his license due to allegations of unethical practices. Dr. Semir had no further recommendations, so I dropped the subject.

But my question about death still haunted me.

At this point, Scott was the only one with whom I had shared my near-death experience. The experience was precious to me, and I didn't want anybody tainting it. The dreams of going to hell were terrifying, but I was worried I would be locked up in an insane asylum if I told anyone about them. So, I tried to put the whole experience out of my mind and move on with life. I thought it wouldn't be too difficult, because we had a lot of things going on. Scott and I had recently qualified for a pizza franchise in our hometown of Granger, Indiana, so we were busy putting our two stores in South Dakota up for sale and planning a move.

After we moved to Granger, Indiana, the near-death experience and the dreams of hell were so vivid I couldn't keep them out of my mind. I thought about them often. In fact, it seemed the more I tried not to think about them, the more I did. The desire for answers burned in my heart every day. I had to know more about the near-death experience and what happens when you die.

Scott and I talked about it and decided I should reach out to a doctor one more time. We looked in the yellow pages and picked one.

When I arrived at my appointment, I planned on wasting no time. At eighty dollars an hour, I didn't bother with pleasantries.

Once seated in front of his desk, I asked him the question point blank.

“I’m here for one reason,” I said. “I want to know what happens to you when you die.”

“Why do you want to know?”

“I’m curious.” I sat back in my chair, knowing I had the rest of the hour to hear the answer.

“Let’s not rush into things so quickly,” the doctor said.

Uh-oh. Here we go again.

The doctor was young and seemed nervous. He began fidgeting—talking in circles around the subject, referring to psychological theories that made no sense. They all seemed to be recycled ideas from his collection of college textbooks.

I tried to bring the conversation back to the original question, but he spent the entire hour pointing to his books and talking about different theories he had learned in school, which had nothing to do, as far as I could make out, with my question.

When he finally quit talking, I asked again. “What happens to you when you die?”

He just stared at me for a moment, then looked up at the clock. “Sorry,” he said. “The time is up.” He stood and walked out of his office leaving me sitting there, alone. No next appointment. Nothing.

I felt betrayed.

Was I ever going to learn the answer to my question?

I walked out of the office into the pelting rain. I didn't even run to escape the downpour. Drenched by the time I reached the car, I drove home hopeless.

He doesn't know the answer. Nobody does.

Chapter 8

The Farm

WHEN I ARRIVED HOME, Scott was anxious to hear about my appointment. "How'd it go?"

"Strike three," I said.

"No luck, huh?"

"Psychologists are out." I threw the mail on the table.

"What happened?"

"He didn't answer my question."

"Maybe we should search on our own," Scott suggested. "I have something that will cheer you up." He waved a book back and forth in front of me.

My hope started to return.

I began reading the book on wilderness survival and awareness that very night. The author talked about a spiritual connection with a higher power in a wilderness setting. The story told of two boys mentored by a Native American elder. They learned how to navigate by using nature in the spiritual realm.

What I read spoke to my soul, and I couldn't put the book down until the end. I noticed a phone number in the back of the book with an advertisement about a school that taught wilderness awareness and philosophy classes.

I was drawn to call the number.

If the doctors couldn't answer my question, then maybe the school could.

I learned two openings were left for the beginning course. The only problem was the class started in two weeks. I tried to find someone to go with me, but no one could on such short notice. I didn't let that stop me. I booked one of the spots and started organizing my bags. I danced around the house while I packed. After talking to one of the instructors and learning more about the classes, I was convinced that this time I was going to find some answers.

When I arrived for the week-long course, butterflies fluttered in my stomach. *What was I getting myself into?* The topic was wilderness survival and awareness, but I had no idea what that actually meant.

The registration table was set up outside. Shelley, the camp director, pointed to the big red barn behind her. "Sleeping quarters are in the loft."

After thanking her, I quickly claimed my spot and unloaded my gear. I was the first to arrive as it was late morning and the class did not officially start until six that evening.

"Can I explore the property?" I asked.

"Sure," Shelley said. "Just keep the barn in sight and you'll be okay."

The camp was located on a farm next to a beautiful creek that meandered across rolling meadows surrounded by thick forests. Other than the farmhouse on the property, no other houses were in view. Feeling anxious after the twelve-hour drive the day before, I walked the grounds, enjoying the cool air and far-seeing view. After a bit, I found a grassy spot next to a stream and sat near a tree.

The sound of water trickling over rocks soothed me. I leaned back and took a deep breath, trying to identify all the different earthy smells. Newly cut grass and lilacs mingled with the scent of fresh hay. Spring was in full bloom.

In truth, I was probably more anxious about what I might discover this week than I was from the long drive. Dave, the main instructor, seemed amazing in his books. He talked a lot about having a sixth sense and spiritual awareness. I had high hopes I would soon have my questions answered. I was going to learn how to get back to the spiritual realm—the place I had not wanted to leave during my near-death experience. I was anxious to get back to the place where all my senses had been awakened and heightened to extraordinary levels. Just thinking about it made my heart race, but I also felt a bit afraid. I did not want to go back to hell, and that seemed part of the deal.

I forced myself not to think about it anymore. I would know soon enough. I leaned back and emptied myself of all thoughts other than the myriad sounds and smells around me. After a few hours, I walked the long, curvy path back to the barn and wondered what the teacher would be like in real life.

Most of Dave's experiences took place in a wilderness setting and revolved around survival skills. I felt more comfortable in the woods than in the city, so at least we had that in common. But I knew little about survival skills and wondered if I would fit in with the type of people who focused on such things. I pictured a class full of military-type guys, with me sitting like an awkward duck among them. But as I entered the classroom, which was really just a rustic part of the barn, I was met with a wonderful surprise.

Several people already were seated on planks that served as benches scattered throughout the room. My classmates ranged in age from very young to quite old and appeared to come from every walk of life. I sat next to a grandmother named Mary. She was from Texas and had always wanted to take a wilderness survival course. Next to her sat a teenager named Paul. He had hitchhiked all the way from California and was soon entertaining us with tales of his many adventures along the way.

I was one of forty people enrolled in the course.

Two instructors—Derek and Ben—went over our agenda, then finally introduced the main teacher. Dave didn't look at all like

I had pictured. I had expected someone with long hair and a full beard dressed in buckskins and furs, the typical mountain man you see on TV. Instead, Dave was clean cut with short hair and a mustache. He wore jeans and a T-shirt. He was built like someone you would see in the Special Forces, and he talked in a deep, commanding voice.

My heart quickened. Would this man be my path back to that spiritual realm?

I was expecting full survival conditions right from the beginning, but I was relieved to learn this course taught the skills necessary to move on to that level of survival.

"We'll teach you how to build shelters," Dave explained, "gather food and water, and in addition to how to make a fire and cook primitively, you'll learn to track animals as well as humans, set traps, and make your own rope."

Make my own rope. I wondered how we would even begin such a task. But then my ears perked.

"In addition to physical skills," Dave said, "we will be teaching you some spiritual awareness techniques."

I sat on the edge of my bench, hanging onto every word. I was so ready! I just knew I would find the answer to my question: what happens to you when you die?

I could imagine myself returning home to share my answer with Scott. Maybe I could even lead him to experience what I had experienced. The thought gave me new determination. I would give my all to this class, learning everything possible from the most mundane to the toughest challenges.

This was what I was born for, and I could not wait.

Chapter 9

Surprised

AN ENORMOUS CLANG WOKE ME the next morning. I jumped out of bed and realized they were using a cowbell to summon us. I quickly dressed and headed down to breakfast, worried we would have to eat pine nuts or some other strange thing. Instead, I was delighted to discover a regular breakfast of scrambled eggs and oatmeal waiting on rustic tables of slabbed wood. In the days before cell phones, the only modern convenience—a payphone— hung in the barn.

Back in the classroom, Dave explained our agenda for the day. "The number one thing people die from is exposure," he said. "So, the first thing we will do is learn to build a shelter."

I was surprised at how easy it was to build a simple shelter. We started with a debris hut that could be made out of anything. We used leaves and pine needles because they were everywhere on the farm. We did everything as a group so we could all gain a little experience.

Although we worked as a group, Mary, the grandmother from Texas, teamed with me when it came time to gather the debris. We were not allowed to use modern tools like rakes and shovels, so my fingers were the rake while Mary used her jacket to gather the piles I made. When the jacket was full, we carried it to the shelter the class was building, which made the job less taxing. Like me, Mary took the course seriously. Together we excelled.

"In future courses," Dave always reminded us, "you will be doing this on your own. So, you better practice!"

I took his advice to heart.

After a lunch of tuna sandwiches, we lined up in a grassy field. We were going to learn how to fox walk in wide-angle vision.

Dave explained the art of fox walking. "Slowing down and having awareness is vital." He went on to explain how fox walking is a slow, quiet way of moving through nature.

Barefoot with knees bent, we placed the outside of our foot down, rolling the rest flat before adding any weight. The class made very little noise walking this way.

The next training on wide-angle vision was quite challenging at first. We raised our hands and arms out to our sides until we could see all the fingers on both hands wiggling simultaneously. We also had to see the bottom of our feet and the sky above while looking straight ahead. This training taught us how to use our peripheral vision and even expand it.

I started to get the hang of it after several minutes. I could see so much more than usual while staying in wide-angle vision and fox walking. The only time we were allowed to focus was if something caught our attention. We could look at it for a moment, but then we had to jump right back into wide-angle vision. Before long, my brain waves slowed, and I started to become one with nature. I felt in sync with my surroundings while flowing in that rhythm. I walked the length of the field in that flow.

After an hour, it was time to make a fire with sticks. We learned the bow drill first. Paul, the young man who hitchhiked from California, got his fire going right away. I wondered if he had done this before. Mary and I were not so lucky. We both bumbled with the technique. Paul encouraged us and tried to give pointers.

With some adjustments, Mary and I were at least able to create some smoke. *This is going to take a while.*

I didn't care. I would give it as much time as it needed.

I never was able to make a fire during that first class. It wasn't from lack of effort. The process required technique, strength, and endurance. With all the other physical demands of the course, I just didn't have the strength that first week.

During supper, several students packed up and left. How could they give up so soon?

We were told this was common for the first class. People envision different expectations of what a wilderness survival and awareness class will be like. Some people are never prepared for the physical demands or the hands-on approach used in the first class.

I could not give up, because my goals differed from theirs. If I could make it through this course, I could find answers. Though, I couldn't help but wonder if I had what it took to make it through the entire week.

That night, instead of resting, we began our training on tracking. The instructors lectured the first hour while I frantically took notes. Then the leaders had us scoot our benches back. They pulled a huge piece of plywood up from the floor. I was utterly surprised to see an enormous sandbox.

We began to practice. First, we started with our own tracks. Dave walked across the sandbox, explaining all the nuances. We learned about direction, speed, and type. Then we graduated to clay casts of animal prints.

By the time I climbed the ladder to the loft, it was after midnight. I crawled to my sleeping bag, I didn't bother to wash up or change my clothes. When my head hit the pillow, I was out.

Chapter 10

The Tribe

I WASN'T THE ONLY ONE who slept in the clothes they had worn the day before, as my classmates climbed out of sleeping bags for breakfast. The only bathing facility was the creek that ran through the property. Few chose to bathe that morning. We had to eat quickly, because we faced a packed schedule.

Day three focused on cooking and finding water and food. Gathering water and making it safe to drink topped the list. We needed something to boil the water in, so we learned a technique called bowl burning.

We built a campfire and let it burn until plenty of coals glowed red-hot. Then we made a pair of tongs by bending a live branch. Each person was given split firewood, and we used our tongs to place the coals on the flat side. I blew on the coals with a hollow reed to burn a hole in the firewood. Then we all joined together to burn a bowl in a large stump. This would become our kettle for making soup.

For our next task, we collected three small- to medium-sized stones that we would heat and drop in the water to make it boil. I was excited to see how this would work.

"We are going to use these stones for boiling water," Dave said. "But be warned! Never gather stones from creeks or standing water. If water gets into the stone through cracks and you heat it, it could explode."

Mary and I looked at each other with wide eyes.

"Getting hit by a flying piece of rock could be lethal," Dave said.

To this day, I never collect rocks in wet places.

I decided to gather my stones in the meadow far from the stream. Because I wanted to get as close to nature as possible and experience the full scope of Dave's class, I decided to name my stones. I called them Toby, Charles, and Max. One rock became Charles because I wanted a royal name in the mix. Max was my childhood tomcat, and Toby reminded me of a hobbit, which was perfect for our primitive setting.

I carried my stones back to the campfire, where I used my tongs to place them on the coals. When the stones glowed red, I placed them in the wood pot I had made. The water instantly boiled.

"Can you believe it, Mary?" I hung the tongs on a branch.

"This is so cool," she agreed. "I feel like a real wild woman."

We both stood there with big smiles, watching the water boil. When it slowed, we replaced the cooled stones with hot ones.

When we finished our training, we knew how to rid our water of parasites and how to boil meat with edible plants.

During lunch, Ken, a chiropractic student, volunteered to give free back adjustments. He seemed rather barbaric and harsh with his procedure, so I passed. Personalities were beginning to surface. Some, like Mary, were more in tune with nature and flowed in that rhythm, while others stomped around crashing through brush, trying to conquer the wilderness.

I was glad Mary and I had found each other. I did all I could to avoid the wilderness conquerors. They ate their lunch while standing around the fire, regaling each other with their past conquests. Mary and I ate in silence, enjoying nature.

After lunch, Derek showed us how to make snares, deadfall traps, spears, and rabbit sticks. A rabbit stick is a club used to hunt rabbits and other small game. All we had to do was find a good stick and either weight it or carve it to fit our needs. Then we found a long, straight stick and carved a point on the end to make a spear.

Derek stalked along the banks of the creek, teaching us how to use our spears to catch fish. The fish were scared by the time we arrived, so Mary and I came up with none. But we still enjoyed learning how to use our spears.

Knowing where to set the traps was a whole new way of thinking. You have to be the animal and think like it thinks.

First, Dave taught about animal trails and runs and how to find them. Then, Ben showed us how to hear concentric rings in the wilderness. Animals put out concentric circles as warning signals throughout the forest or meadow when danger lurks. One species makes a call that sets off a call from another. This important lesson sharpened our awareness skills. I loved sitting in the woods listening to all the animal sounds.

As we sat alone in our different spots, Ben walked through the woods and meadow making noises. I listened for how the different animals, mainly birds, would send warning calls. Then, other animals would send calls. As I listened, I found myself falling into deeper states of awareness, which amplified my hearing and sense of smell. Even though Ben was across the meadow, I could smell his deodorant.

I could hear individual birds, as well as squirrels, give their warning calls. It reminded me of listening to an orchestra and yet hearing each instrument. In a short time, I could tell what kind of threat was coming. The animal calls would rise to a crescendo then quiet back down after the danger had passed. I found it hard to pull myself away for dinner.

Everyone seemed calmer during our meal, even the wilderness conquerors. Sitting in nature for hours has that effect on people.

For the first time, I felt all of us were becoming somewhat of a tribe even though we didn't really know each other. I could see this was part of something bigger. If all this could happen in just a few days, I wondered what amazing things were ahead. I had grown up in a big family, but I had never before experienced such community with strangers. Perhaps, there was more for me here than simply finding the answers to my questions.

I wanted the full experience.

After dinner, Dave talked about the importance of making cordage. Having some kind of rope is an enormous help in any situation.

I've never looked at my shoelaces the same way again.

The rest of the night was dedicated to practicing. We used twine, string, and yarn that night, to get the twisting technique down before we learned how to do the same with plant fibers.

The day had been exciting and full. When class finally ended, most of us hit the sack. My goal was to try to rise before the cowbell, so I could take a private dip in the creek.

Chapter 11

A Deadly Plant

AT SUNRISE THE NEXT MORNING, I stepped into the creek. Within minutes, my feet and legs grew numb. Shivering while I lathered up my hair and body, I braced myself for the final rinse, which involved a total dunking in frigid water.

I dressed and hurried back to the barn where I sat next to a gal from Canada named Frances while we made cordage. I was curious if Canadians handled the outdoors better than Americans.

“Do you spend a lot of time outdoors?” I asked as I twisted the inner bark with my fingers. The scent of cedar filled the space around us.

“I do spend quite a bit of time in the wilderness,” Frances said. “Several national parks are nearby.” She held up her piece of cordage that now looked like rope. “But it’s the spiritual awareness part that intrigues me.”

“Me too!” *Wow! Someone else is interested in similar things.*

I was too nervous to ask her any more questions, but I hoped to learn more later. We both practiced making cordage until breakfast was ready. When I wasn't with Mary, I ate meals by myself. I preferred to observe people rather than communicate with them, because I didn't know what to say. This was all so new to me. I didn't want to appear an odd duck.

Our next class identified plants. I never knew so many of the plants I considered weeds were edible or medicinal. We also learned to identify poisonous ones and plants that may have negative outcomes on our bodies. We passed around live samples, photos, and guidebooks. We spent hours going through the guides and notes, and then we studied plants and inner bark that would make the best cordage.

At this point, I was on information overload and appreciated our lunch break. After we ate peanut butter and jelly sandwiches, we were placed in groups of five.

Beginning our next training in awareness, each group stood around a plant and closed their eyes. We were told to focus on the plant and see what thoughts or sensations arose. Dave also warned us not to taste anything.

I closed my eyes and waited.

A young gal, Melissa, in the group next to us, started heaving.

I opened one eye and looked her direction.

She calmed after a few seconds, but then she took several steps away from the plant. It was hemlock—a deadly plant if eaten.

I was amazed she could experience such a violent reaction simply through awareness.

"That was weird," whispered Bobby.

"Yeah," said James.

I remained silent, wondering if I would ever be that aware.

Our group plant was milkweed. I knew the flowers were edible if cooked and best if made into a milkweed fritter, which is why I probably smelled and tasted fried chicken when I focused on the plant. Monarch butterflies use the flowers as a food source. I thought that was cool, and it gave me a warm fuzzy feeling.

We were told to never rely only on the awareness technique one hundred percent. Instead, we could use it in addition to the guidebook to help us tune into the plant kingdom. I found the technique quite interesting, because I had read that plants can give off signals and scents for self-protection against predators. I wondered if becoming more aware allowed me to pick up on those nuances. More pieces of the puzzle were coming together, and I recognized more dimensions and aspects to my question than I initially thought.

The instructors watched diligently as we gathered plants for our salad that evening. Each of us would only eat a few forkfuls, just enough to give us a taste. The teachers were thorough and went through each gathered plant to ensure nothing harmful had made its way into the mix.

Late in the afternoon, an ice cooler was opened in front of us, revealing more than forty bluegill and other sunfish. The smell filled the barn. It reminded me of walking through an open fish market on a warm day, and this afternoon approached ninety degrees.

We were each told to take a fish, and then we learned how to clean and prepare it for the open fire. We had no fancy kitchen in which to work. A piece of firewood served as a prep table, and a garden hose provided our only source of clean water. We built a big campfire with plenty of red-hot coals. We each cooked our fish to our own liking. The fish and the wild plants comprised our dinner.

About an hour into the evening lecture, Sarah, who sat on the front row, ran out of the barn and started throwing up. We could all hear her.

Dave, the instructor, made a joke. “I guess she didn’t like what I said.”

We all laughed, but it wasn’t long before a few others joined her. Most of us made it through the session, including me, but in the wee hours of the morning, several of us ran out of the barn to puke.

The plants didn’t get to me. The fish did. My fish was underdone, which surprised me. I didn’t anticipate a problem, because people eat sushi all the time without getting sick. Evidently, one must cook everything extremely well done when in the wild. Undercooking fish in the wild was a rookie mistake. I'm glad I wasn't in an actual survival situation before I learned this valuable lesson.

Food poisoning is no fun.

Chapter 12

The Sweat Lodge

LUCKILY, THE FOOD POISONING didn't last long. Oatmeal, the next morning's breakfast, was the perfect meal.

During our first session on the fourth day, we worked on brain tanning a deer hide. The pig brains used to tan the hide made me a bit queasy, but I pushed through. When we finished the brain tanning, we placed the hide in a smoker. Then, we started working on constructing a sweat lodge.

A sweat lodge is a domed shelter with a small opening facing east that one crawls through to get inside. I was excited about the sweat lodge. I knew many people received visions and insights there, and I was sure I would get one as well.

This is what I came for. I was nervous and excited at the same time.

First, we gathered large stones to be heated in the campfire until they glowed red. When hot enough, we placed these stones in a pit in the center of the lodge.

After supper, we all headed to the sweat lodge in our swimsuits. It happened to be a full moon, and the skies were clear. We crawled in and formed a circle around the red-hot rocks. I was one of the last people to enter the lodge, and I made sure to sit close to the door, as I wasn't sure what to expect and wanted an easy way out.

We had been told there would be four rounds where the leader would pour water over the rocks to create steam while we sat in silence. Steam wafted like a sauna but was more intense. The leader asked questions, but I don't remember a single one. I had my own agenda between rounds on which to reflect. I was sure I was going to have a spiritual experience.

Each round of water pouring was supposed to slow our brain waves and take us deeper into the different states of awareness. The four states progressed in this order: beta, alpha, theta, and delta. Delta went the deepest, but we were told few attained this level while conscious.

The sweat lodge was hotter than I expected. After two rounds, I couldn't take the heat, so I crawled out. Already in a deep awareness state, I laid on my back in the grass just outside the door, staring up at the sky.

A colorful halo stretched around the moon. As I stared at the light, it reminded me of the brilliant star that drew me in my near-death experience. Before I knew what was happening, I was lifted back into that place. I only caught a glimpse, but enough to remind me of everything I received the first time. I was one with my surroundings, and my senses became heightened until I knew everything. I understood everything in that moment. The knowledge was more spiritual than intellectual. It nurtured; it was caring and loving. Every part of me, from the core outward, was affected. I was unconditionally accepted for who I was. No pain, no shame, no sense of finiteness.

I could have stayed there forever.

But the sweat lodge ended, and the students started to come out. They remained quiet, for which I was grateful, but the interruption took me out of the moment.

I continued to stare at the moon while breathing in the aroma of warm grass until well after midnight.

Chapter 13

Sixth Sense

ON THE LAST DAY OF THE COURSE, which ended at noon, I rose before the cowbell and packed my gear before breakfast. I had received so much information this week that my brain was on overload. I was ready for some time to process everything I had learned. The thought of sharing it with Scott was also exciting.

Sitting up front next to my Canadian friend Frances during the morning lecture, I asked, "Are you excited about the other classes the school offers?"

"Yes. I'm going to sign up for his philosophy course this fall."

I studied the upcoming course schedule and decided to sign up for the next five courses, including Advanced Skills, Advanced Tracking and Awareness, Philosophy I and II, and Winter Survival.

I said goodbye to Mary, thinking this would probably be the last time I would see her. Her family had given this course to her as a gift.

"I enjoyed this class," she said, "but I'm not physically able to do the more challenging courses."

I swung my backpack over my shoulder and walked the dirt driveway toward my car. When I slipped into the driver's seat, I fumbled with the keys and turned on the windshield wipers by mistake. *Had it only been a week since I had been in my car? It felt more like a month.*

Driving the narrow road, I kept seeing things out of my peripheral vision. It about drove me crazy, like looking through a Coke bottle where everything in the middle is narrowed, and the edges are expanded. The road seemed too skinny to maneuver. I felt out of control at thirty miles an hour.

Once I reached the highway, everything moved too fast; there was so much to see. Then, on top of it all, people started honking at me. My senses became overloaded and started to shut down.

Girl, you gotta get hold of yourself before you reach the interstate.

I was telling myself a lot of things, trying to quench the rising panic. After forcing myself not to see in wide-angle vision, I increased my speed to 45 miles an hour. I concentrated on focusing straight ahead, so I wouldn't go crazy with all the movement happening around me. Once on the interstate, my shoulders were up to my ear lobes, and I maintained a death grip on the steering wheel. Finally, I was able to do fifty-five miles per hour, and people stopped honking.

Once I hit the Blue Ridge Mountains, my shoulders lowered, and I loosened my grip. Everything slowed back down to the wilderness rhythm. The night sky fell like a blanket around me, and I went back into wide-angle vision. I saw more wildlife alongside the road than I had ever noticed before. I sensed them before I saw them. I even sensed a large herd of deer around the next bend, and there they were! I experienced this "sixth sense" all the way home.

When I arrived late that night, I woke Scott. We talked until morning about everything I learned. Somewhere in our conversation, I realized I could never again return to my old way of life. I would never see things the way I once had. I didn't want to return to my hectic lifestyle, fearing I would lose my connection to the spiritual world. I had gone deep, but I wanted to go deeper yet, and I sure didn't want to lose what I already had gained.

Chapter 14

Debris Huts

Granger, Indiana, June 1990

AUNT BETSY WAS THE FIRST PERSON I told about my wilderness survival training, besides Scott. She lived close, in the same town of Granger, and was only a few years older than me. I sat on a green plaid couch in her living room with the smell of coffee drifting around us.

“Tell me all about it,” she said.

“It wasn’t anything like I thought it would be.”

Betsy leaned forward in her chair, tucking a wisp of sandy blonde hair behind her ear. “What kind of things did you do?”

“One thing,” I said, “is I made a spear to catch fish out of the creek.”

“Did you catch any?” Betsy also enjoyed fishing.

“No.” I laughed. “But I had fun trying.”

"What else did you do?"

I leaned back on the couch, trying to think of some of my favorite things that would appeal to Betsy. "We made a protective shelter out of debris."

"Really?" Her bluish-green eyes brightened. "I would like to do that."

"You can join me," I said.

Betsy clapped her hands together. "I would love that. Where do you want to do it?"

It didn't take but a moment to answer. "Let's go to Mom and Dad's house this weekend. We can build our shelters, and then we can spend the night in them."

Betsy stood. "I'm so excited!"

"Me too." What fun to have someone to share my new skills with.

I left Betsy's and drove to my parents' house to ask permission. I was hoping my mother would be as excited as Betsy, so I told her what we wanted to do.

She barely looked up from her gardening. "I take it you had a good time at your class?"

"Oh yes! It was amazing. I learned all kinds of things about how to survive and some really cool spiritual awareness techniques from Native American cultures."

Sharing with my mom brought the whole experience back, as if I was reliving the entire week. Before I knew it, my words were coming out in a tumble.

"We did a sweat lodge where I learned how to slow down my brain waves, and then I came out and stared at the moon, and suddenly I knew things I had never been taught. It was awesome!"

Mom dropped her garden tool and looked up with wide eyes.

That's when I realized she just wasn't getting it. How could anyone who hadn't experienced it get it? This conversation would need to continue another time.

After a few seconds of silence, she picked up her garden tool and simply said, "You and Betsy can build your shelters here."

With the weekend still a few days away, I decided to read another of Dave's books. This one talked about his personal stories and offered teachings on spiritual awareness in nature. I read the entire book before meeting Betsy and couldn't wait to share some of it with her.

On a clear summer day, we started building our debris huts. I showed Betsy how to find sticks and debris and put them together into something she could crawl into for protection. She seemed to possess a knack for it right from the beginning, while the perfectionist part of me kept getting in my way. The task had seemed easy when forty of us were building a hut together, but now I struggled with making the frame too big and steep. The debris kept falling off the sides. We worked all morning with very little talk, both of us focused on what we were doing.

When I finished, my shelter was the shape of an old Boy Scout tent, not exactly what I had hoped. I was trying to make it more rounded, similar to what we had done in class. I looked at Betsy's and saw a perfect cocoon.

That's an interesting shape.

Betsy emerged with a big smile, and her entire body covered with pieces of debris. We were both drenched in sweat.

"That's a lot of work," Betsy said, brushing herself off.

"Yes, and there's a storm brewing. I sure hope our shelters keep us dry."

Betsy looked up at the sky where the clouds were piling up. "We'll find out tonight."

We both laughed.

Mom called us in to dinner, where I talked about what I had read in Dave's latest book. My parents listened while Betsy and I did most of the talking.

"Dave wrote about all these ceremonies he and his best friend did with their old Indian friend they called Grandfather," I said.

"What else did they do?" Betsy asked.

"They pretended to be Apache scouts and would set traps for each other. Then they would hide in the woods and find each other by traveling outside their bodies."

Betsy's eyes grew wide. "Really?"

"They would also go back in time and observe what different tribal ancestors did."

"Cool," Betsy said. "But how is that even possible?"

"I don't know, but I'm going to find out when I take more of his classes. He is an amazing storyteller. I just lose myself in his books." I didn't tell her it was easy for me to believe extraordinary things were possible after my near-death experience. I still hadn't told anyone, other than Scott, about the power of that unknown realm. But I wasn't about to discount anybody's story after what I had been through.

"This is going to be so fun!" Betsy said.

My parents remained silent throughout our entire conversation. After dinner, Betsy and I headed to the woods and crawled into our debris shelters.

The storm had passed to the north, so I hoped we were in the clear. I was almost asleep when the rain hit. It wasn't heavy, but it found every hole in my hut, and there were many. I was wet and cold within minutes. When shivers began to rack my body, I decided to go in the house and sleep.

The next morning, when I came outside, Betsy emerged from her shelter completely dry. "I slept really good," Betsy said. "How about you?

I shook my head. "Not so much."

I didn't want to tell her what had happened, but I ended up confessing. "You get an "A" this time Betsy."

She beamed.

"But I totally flunked. Let's go see what I did wrong."

After comparing, we both decided a cocoon shape was better. Less was more and easier. I had some work to do if I was going to excel in the second, more advanced class.

In the following weeks, Betsy and I talked about making peace pipes, drums, and rattles. She loved everything about Native American culture and wanted to experience the state of awareness I had talked about during dinner. I promised we would do more after I returned from the next class.

I had to take the courses in the order of prerequisites, but I didn't mind. The classes challenged me to grow and learn new things about nature awareness and myself. The next course was two classes in one, where we would spend two weeks in the wilderness. The first week would focus on survival, and the second week on tracking and spiritual awareness and teachings.

I could hardly wait.

Chapter 15

Survival

Pine Barrens Base Camp, New Jersey, fall 1990

I WAITED IN THE DESIGNATED PARKING LOT for my ride. Not just any vehicle could travel the dirt trails through the pine barrens that led to camp. The journey required a four-wheel drive truck. When it arrived, four of us threw our gear into the truck bed and climbed in. Being a farm girl, I was used to riding in the back of an open truck. We slowly bumped along through a pine forest. Light filtered through the trees, making it look otherworldly. I loved the way the pine needles sparkled in the sunshine.

Twenty minutes later, we reached our destination. Base camp consisted of two primitive structures, a makeshift kitchen made of weathered wood and a large hogan covered in greenhouse plastic. A simple trail separated them. Almost everything about camp was primitive and rustic. This was going to be the real deal.

Ben greeted us as we climbed out of the truck.

"It's great to see you again," I said, reaching for my gear.

"You can set up tents anywhere within a quarter mile of camp," Ben said. "Put your utensils on the wooden plank next to the kitchen." He also pointed out that the large hogan would be our meeting place. He called it the Thunder Dome.

We were allowed to set up tents and use them the first few days, as we needed time to build shelters and make the grass mats that would be our sleeping bags for the week.

The camp was in the pine barrens of New Jersey near the ocean. I wandered through the trees, looking for a place to set up my pup tent. The summer sun stood high in the sky, and the smell of pine drifted from the trees. I had never been in a forest quite like this one. The sky painted a blue backdrop, and the soil underneath was a combination of sand and dirt. Very little vegetation, just small shrub brush, grew about calf high. I found a little clearing next to a pine tree and assembled my tent. Then, I grabbed my bowl and spoon and walked back to the main camp.

I had just placed my utensils on the makeshift planked table outside the kitchen area when a student came up to me. "I hear we are only twelve miles from the ocean," he said. He introduced himself as Brad. "This is my first time camping in the woods. I live on the forty-fourth floor of a high-rise in New York City."

"Wow!" I said. "And you chose this to be your first camping experience?"

"Crazy, I know." He chuckled. "But I wanted to do something like this my entire life. Being a stockbroker, I never get a chance to spend time in nature, and I wanted an adventure involving the outdoors."

Another student joined us. "I'm Patty from Colorado, and I spend all my free time in the outdoors."

"Must be nice," Brad mumbled.

"I'm excited to see the cedar swamps," I said.

Patty smiled. "Me too."

Brad pointed to the path. "Let's go have a look. Right down this path next to the creek, there's a dock we can stand on. From there, we can see the cedars."

Patty and I followed Brad. He had arrived the night before and had time to explore. The landscape suddenly changed when we neared the creek, which flowed only three hundred yards from camp. Thin willow saplings and other leafy weeds grew next to the narrowing trail. The air became humid and swampy, smelling of rich earth. Immediately, flies and mosquitoes swarmed us.

We raised our voices against the buzzing.

"The ground is all mucky now," Patty said.

I looked down at my bare feet. "It's oozing between my toes."

"We're almost there," Brad assured.

We continued to swat mosquitoes and navigate the muck until we finally stood at the end of the dock. The water was clear with a slight amber tint. The winding stream separated the sandy pine areas from the cedar swamps. The cedars across the stream towered in comparison to the pine trees.

They reminded me of the California Redwoods, just not as tall. "This is amazing!"

"Let's cross the creek and explore the swamps," Patty said.

"Better not," Brad said. "There are areas of dangerous quicksand, and the banks are so mucky you sink up to your waist."

"Then how do you get across?" I asked.

Brad smiled. "You have to float on your stomach on top of the mud and paddle your way in."

I couldn't picture how I could paddle my way through mud and muck without getting sucked down. "This week is certainly going to be challenging."

We hurried back to camp, not wanting to be late for our first meeting.

The last of the students had arrived, and we all met at the Thunder Dome. I sat near the front on the dirt floor next to a woman my age, who called herself Lou. She spoke with a European accent I couldn't quite place.

"Before we start," Ben said, "I want to take this group down to the creek and show you where to collect water."

We all headed out the door, but instead of following the path toward the swamp, we veered left and followed a path that took us farther upstream. The ground was firm and the water easier to reach.

"This is where we gather drinking water," Ben said. "You can bathe and swim downstream by the dock. After filling the jugs with water, put two of these tablets in each one and let them sit for a few hours. If you don't do this, you could get giardia."

"Giardia! I don't even know what that is." I looked at Lou.

"It's a parasite that'll make you sick," she said.

"Really?" I said. "Where are you from?"

"Sweden."

"That explains the accent," I said.

Ben let us taste some water he had already treated. The water was brown with tannin from the cedar tree roots, and it tasted bitter. I had to hold my nose to get it down and wondered how I would make it through the entire two weeks. We walked back to the Thunder Dome, where Dave was ready to start class. Fifty of us sat on the sandy ground and listened while Dave began to speak.

"This is going to be a physically challenging week," he said. "I want you to go out and pick a place to build your debris hut and, remember, ninety percent of your success is choosing the right place."

Then we were up again and out the door. I watched as Patty chose a spot with mostly pine needles. Growing up in deciduous forests, I preferred a place that offered a combination of both leaves and pine needles. Brad chose a location that was sunny with little debris.

We were supposed to search out the right spot. I wandered for quite some time, but the perfectionist part of me could never find the perfect place. Finally, afraid of falling behind, I made myself pick a spot with pine needles and leaves and called it done.

At dinner, we were fed spaghetti and told this would be the best meal of the week. I wondered what that meant, since the spaghetti wasn't all that great.

After supper, Ben led us out of camp about a quarter of a mile, where he placed us in one long line with ten feet between each person. The black night kept us from seeing anything more than three feet away, yet we were told to blindfold ourselves.

Seriously?

"This is an important exercise," Ben said. "You'll appreciate it later."

I wasn't so sure, but I was willing to give it a try.

After we were all blindfolded, Ben gave more instructions. "Your goal is to walk back to camp by following a drumbeat. Walk slowly and steadily, leaving the blindfold on, trying not to trip in the thick underbrush or hit any trees."

The drumbeat thundered every five seconds, echoing through the forest.

As my classmates crashed through the brush, I feared being left behind. I raised my arms and tried to move faster, but the underbrush, like tentacles on an octopus, grabbed at my feet. I fell to the ground. I stood back up and lifted my feet high, trying to go over the brush, but I kept getting tangled in the underbrush. Nothing seemed to work until I began to inch my feet along the ground.

I took a deep breath. As I became more aware of my physical body and surroundings, I heard the drumbeat echoing rhythmically through the woods.

After a few tries, I fell into more of a meditative state and instinctively found little paths to move along through the underbrush, remaining untangled. I could smell campfire smoke drifting through the air as the drumbeat grew louder. I was getting close.

Then, suddenly, I felt a presence in front of me.

I brought my hands up and placed them on something rough and sticky. My fingers searched until I discovered grooves in a cylinder-type object. "A pine tree," I whispered.

I had felt the presence of the tree before I hit it. Now, this was getting exciting!

Moving a little faster with more confidence, I stayed in the moment, and my other senses came alive, making up for the lack of vision. I sensed every tree as if someone guided me. I was learning to see in a different way, and it worked better than using my physical eyes.

I walked straight to the drummer and took off my blindfold. “I did it!” I shrieked.

The other students who had already made it back smiled up at me.

I clenched my fists in the air, knowing there was no turning back. Never in my wildest dreams did I ever think I could experience something like this.

Chapter 16

The Reward

I WAS STILL EXCITED the following day when I came out of my tent for breakfast. It didn't even bother me that the oatmeal was so thick it stuck to the serving spoon when I turned it upside down over my bowl. I had to push it off with my fingers.

I sat on a log next to Lou. "Are you ready for this week?" I asked.

"More than."

I wish that was true for me. I was certainly ready for more of what I had experienced last night, but I wished I had practiced my outdoor skills more.

A loud whistle pierced the forest, commanding our attention. "Class starts in five minutes!" Ben yelled with a deep military voice.

I hurried to the Thunder Dome so I could sit upfront. Lou and Patty followed suit, sitting next to me. While we waited for Dave to arrive, the three of us talked about how we had discovered the school. It turned out we had all learned of the school's existence through reading Dave's books.

We didn't have long to talk, because Dave entered the Dome at a brisk pace. "All right, everyone," he said. "Let's get started."

The Dome went silent, like a calm forest before a thunderstorm. Everyone leaned forward to hear what Dave had to say.

"I want to keep this short as you have a big day ahead of you."

"It's already hot," I whispered, "and it's still early."

"I'm not used to this humidity," Lou said.

Patty chuckled, more out of nerves than humor. Being from Colorado, she wasn't used to the humidity either.

Dave kept his talk short and sweet, informing us that the first task of the day was to build our debris huts. He gave us all morning to work on them.

The three of us wished each other luck as we headed out.

I gathered sticks for the frame as I made my way to the spot I had chosen. Instead of making it small and cocoon-shaped like Aunt Betsy's, mine ended up like a pup tent again. I figured if I had to spend the week in it, more room would be better, but I soon realized there wasn't enough debris around me to fully cover the structure to the depth I needed.

"Not again," I mumbled. "Do you have any extra debris?" I yelled to Patty.

"Not really. I'm having enough trouble covering my own hut."

This is just going to have to do. I lashed together some twigs with debris for my door. When finished, my hut looked like an old broken-down miniature shack. I was disappointed, but there was no time to start over.

Lunch was tracker stew, which consisted of an onion, diced carrots, and potatoes boiled in water. That's it—a far cry from Mom's home cooking full of spices and condiments. Here there were no condiments or side dishes, and the stew definitely could have used some salt.

I could barely choke it down.

"Get used to it," Wayne, the main cook, said. "That's what you're getting for the rest of the week. Oatmeal in the morning and stew for lunch and dinner."

Brad must have felt the same way about the stew, because he grimaced as he ate. Patty seemed content, and Lou actually looked grateful.

Dave saved us by announcing the next task. "Now, we are going to walk two miles to reach a pond where we will collect reeds to make mats. These will be used in place of a sleeping bag."

I soon realized wearing shoes was a mistake, because beach sand formed the road. My shoes and socks quickly filled. I took my shoes off, but then I had to carry them.

Once we arrived at the pond, we worked as a team to collect enough reeds for everyone. Luckily, the instructors had a truck to haul the reeds. Unfortunately, not everyone fared well. Behind me, people were dropping like flies, and even people next to me suddenly quit and plopped to the ground. I felt bad for them and offered help, but they kept waving me on.

The sun had lowered behind the trees by the time we arrived back at camp. The leaders sent out the truck to gather the stragglers. I was feeling really good about myself, having finished the entire trek. Maybe this was going to turn out okay.

After supper, we were told we could use our sleeping bags in our debris huts this night only, since we needed time to assemble our mats. I grabbed my bag and headed to my hut. My sleeping bag gave me confidence that I wouldn't freeze as I had with Aunt Betsy. Also, the night was humid and still quite warm. I slept soundly that first night.

The whistle blew at the crack of dawn.

I crawled out of my hut and stared at the light rays coming through the pines. I pulled pieces of debris off my damp skin. *It's going to be another hot one today.*

After a pasty breakfast of oatmeal, I went right to work constructing my mat. I found the process easy, putting a small group of reeds together and lashing them with twine until I achieved the desired length.

As I walked toward my hut, I couldn't believe my eyes. Brad's debris hut resembled something Frank Lloyd Wright would have designed—square with a roof on top and an entryway where he stored all his gear. Instead of a simple debris hut, it looked more like a little house. I guess living on the forty-fourth floor of a high rise in downtown New York gives you a different perspective.

"Wow! That looks amazing," I said.

"Thanks. I'm still working on the doors," Brad said.

I laughed. "If we were graded on how it looks, you would get an A-plus in my book."

Patty's hut sat next to mine, so I checked hers out on the way. She wasn't there, but hers seemed more rounded and not as big as Brad's or mine. Tonight would be the test. No sleeping bags allowed. Only grass mats.

A small cold front went through that afternoon, dropping the temperature and humidity. Dark clouds began to form above, and thunder echoed in the distance. I finished my stew as the wind began to pick up. Everyone raced to clean their dinner dishes and hurried to their shelters.

I crawled into my grass mat just before a gentle rain began to fall. Soon, wind howled outside my debris hut; yet I stayed warm and dry inside. *So far, so good.*

But, even though the rain was gentle, it didn't stop for several hours. My hut was better than the first debris hut I had built at my parent's house, but rain still soaked my lower body. Then the wind started to blow. I didn't get too cold, so I stuck it out, but sleep was out of the question.

When I crawled outside the next morning, it looked like a gale had hit. Much of the debris had blown off, and my hut needed some serious patching. I spent most of the morning doing my best to fix the leaks by piling on more debris. With a final pat, I hoped my efforts would be good enough.

The storm front had moved through, and the skies were deep blue again. I felt grateful the temperature had dropped fifteen degrees and there was little humidity.

When we met in the Thunder Dome for our next task, I discovered many students looked "weathered" with a lot of glazed-eyed expressions and interesting hairdos throughout our group. Clearly, my hut was not the only one that had leaked.

We spent the rest of the day making primitive utensils. Bowl burning was easier for me this time after having had a little practice. I made a bowl and spoon that I used for the rest of the course.

As I inhaled the clear and crisp night air, I was excited about finally getting some rest. Wanting to be prepared, I put on several layers of clothes and shimmied into my hut.

I fell asleep fast but woke shivering in the night. The cedar swamps acted like swamp coolers. The cool air drifted through the thin layer of debris, stealing every bit of heat my body tried to create. I curled into a ball for warmth, but my teeth continued to chatter. I pulled the grass mat as tight as possible, but my muscles refused to relax.

After a couple of hours, I was too tired to keep fighting, so I pushed my way out of the hut and walked back to my tent in the moonlight. It would have been a beautiful walk if I had felt good, but good was not even in the picture.

At my tent, I climbed into my sleeping bag and fell fast asleep. The next thing I heard was the whistle call for breakfast.

I wasn't the only one walking to breakfast with my head hung low, which made me feel strangely better. Apparently, others also had given up and returned to their tents.

Lou still wore a big smile on her face.

"You look happy," I said.

"I love living out in the woods," she said.

"Do you do it often?"

She smiled. "Only since I've come to America. I came to take these classes and had little money with no green card to work here. Dave offered me a job as caretaker, so I could attend the classes. I've been living in the woods full time for a month."

"Wow! No wonder you are so at home in the woods. Can you start a fire with the bow drill?" That was primary on my mind because I hadn't succeeded yet.

"Yes."

"Everyone is working on the more advanced methods of starting a fire," I said, "but I can't even start one from the bow drill."

"Tonight, after dinner, I'll help you," Lou offered.

"Awesome! You've got a deal."

After dinner, I practiced starting a fire. Lou came up beside me and gave some pointers. They helped, but I was still coming up short. Several people were practicing, and cedar smoke filled the air. It reminded me of a smoker used for curing meat. Tired but determined, I took a deep breath and relaxed into the rhythm of the motion. When I could push no more, I noticed a tiny coal smoldering in my tinder bundle. Carefully, I picked up the bundle that cradled the coal and began blowing.

"Slow and steady," Lou said. "Blow harder with long blows."

I did as she said. Suddenly, the tinder burst into flames. I dropped it to the ground as a primal scream burst out of me. "Yeeeeess!"

Patty, Lou, and I began dancing around the little fire I had made. I had taken part in something my primitive ancestors had done. I was now part of the mountain women's club.

At the end of the first week, we were rewarded with a breakfast of scrambled eggs. The smell of bacon in the air made my tummy rumble. We were given a day off to rest before the next course started. A few students left, and some new ones came in, but those of us who remained enjoyed a day of fun.

We swam in the creek, lay in the sun, and talked for hours. I sat in a circle with doctors, lawyers, judges, artists, hippies, college students, housemakers, seniors, and foreigners. The class represented every social class and age group, but we all felt equal. We were a tribe, where no one ranked higher than another. I enjoyed being myself and contributing based on who I was born to be instead of what others thought I should be. Being somebody you're not is never satisfying.

I felt a peace I had not experienced before, and I didn't have a care in the world. My mind had dropped into an alpha state of awareness. I couldn't wait to experience the deeper levels offered during our second week. It promised to be everything and more than I had ever dreamed.

Chapter 17

Blindfolded

THE SECOND WEEK STARTED at noon with us sitting on benches while Dave gave instructions. “Now that you’ve had a week of nonstop physical wilderness survival training,” he said, “and many of you learned how challenging that was, this week I’m going to show you how to use your intuition and awareness, which will tremendously advance your skill level.”

Brad sat next to me. “Wish we had this advantage the first week,” he whispered.

“Would have been nice,” I agreed.

“You weren’t ready the first week,” Dave said, almost as if he had heard us. “Most of you came into camp with the world’s problems on your shoulders. You couldn’t even hear a bird sing let alone hear your intuition. You needed the first week to get you prepared for this week.”

Brad gave me a sheepish grin. “He has a point.”

I nodded.

"Now that you're familiar with the camp layout," Dave continued, "I want you all blindfolded until dinner."

Brad and I stared at each other. *Blindfolded for five hours!*

I continued to sit on the bench while I tied on my blindfold and listened for a few moments. People shuffled around. I stayed put and simply listened. Twigs snapped and leaves crunched. I was hearing so much more than before the blindfold. Instructors were talking in the kitchen and helping students find their way. Not being able to use my eyes, my hearing heightened. It seemed as if I could hear everything at once.

Finally, I stood and listened to familiar voices. Lou was laughing, so I slowly walked in her direction. I was so determined to reach her that I forgot about everything else and tripped over a log. I hit the ground hard. Thank God it was sandy soil. Of course, no one saw me fall, because they were all blindfolded, so I didn't need to worry about looking like a fool.

I pulled myself onto the log and sat a moment to recover. Brad and other students talked, but I didn't try to engage because I was still sore from my fall.

This exercise seemed much different from the time before when we were blindfolded in the middle of the night. Although my hearing was enhanced, I didn't feel as in tune as I had before. After several hours, most of us, me included, couldn't take it anymore and removed our blindfolds.

A small group of us wanted to explore the cedar swamps, but we were worried about the quicksand.

"You can go play and practice in the mud pit at the creek," Sarah, one of our helpers, said. "You will only sink up to your waist."

Five of us headed down to the creek. The three guys jumped in first. Patty and I held back to see what would happen. They all sunk immediately to their waists, then Brad went straight down and was completely submerged.

Patty and I grabbed each other in alarm when he didn't reappear.

Then, suddenly, a loud yell filled the air as Brad popped back up, completely covered in mud and looking like a Creature from the Black Lagoon.

The guys howled with laughter while Patty and I took a step back to recover.

"We thought you were a goner," Patty said.

Brad crawled out, smelling like a decomposing swamp. "This pit has a solid bottom," he said, "and is used for camouflaging. You can't hear a thing when you're under the mud."

When the whistle blew, signaling time for dinner, the boys jumped in the creek to wash off while Patty and I hurried back to camp. Spaghetti and garlic bread never tasted so delicious.

The evening lecture was all about exploring the cedar swamps and how to deal with quicksand. The best way to get through quicksand or deep muck was to slither or swim through it on our bellies. However, Dave was quick to point out that, if possible, it was best to go around such places. He ended the night by letting us know we would be spending the next day in the swamps.

We sat around the campfire telling swamp stories. Who would be the first to fall into muck, or worse yet, quicksand? I determined it wouldn't be me. I took comfort in knowing the whole class would be exploring the swamps together. I would let others go first and learn from their mistakes. I went to bed that night feeling confident.

The whistle, which I now called the alarm, went off at 6:00 a.m. The smell of hot grits and scrambled eggs drifted through the air. I ate next to Patty, who also was excited about exploring the swamps. She pointed out, "There are no swamps in Colorado."

"So, what is it like?" I asked.

She talked of the beauty of the mountains and the rugged wild terrain and the herds of elk and other wild animals. The more I listened, the more I felt Colorado calling to me.

"People there are much more open-minded about spiritual things," Patty said.

That did it. I *knew* Colorado was the place for me.

But would Scott agree? I put the thought aside for later, hoping Scott would feel the pull as much as I did.

After breakfast, Patty and I headed to the lecture.

"This morning, I want everyone to find a sit spot in the woods," Dave said. "Stay within a quarter mile of camp, and you can venture into the cedars."

I knew exactly where I was going. I went to the edge of the cedar swamp and worked my way in about thirty feet, where I sat next to a tall cedar. After about twenty minutes, I heard the concentric rings of the animal kingdom begin. First, birds gave off their warning calls, then the squirrels and chipmunks.

Later, we gathered back together as a class and started learning about animal runs and tracking. We spent the rest of the day on these two activities until dinner. After dinner, we were instructed to put on our swimsuits and return barefooted. We were told during supper that we would be doing a blindfold walk after dark.

This time, we were led across the creek and down a narrow logging trail. We then walked through the woods about a quarter mile. We were lined up next to each other, six feet apart, facing camp and told to put on our blindfolds. The drum to guide us beat faintly in the distance.

Tonight's goal was similar to the previous—get back to camp unscathed. However, what lay between us and the drum were several briar patches, thick shrubs, pine trees, and last, but not least, a mud-banked creek to swim across.

We also were instructed to arrive back to camp quietly and without a scratch.

Yeah, okay. That seemed highly unlikely.

Barefoot and with eighty percent of my skin exposed, I felt vulnerable. I experienced doubts, as the briar patch came first. I shivered at the thought of being entangled in that mass of thorns. I began more cautiously than I had during the last blindfold exercise, making sure I accessed that guiding zone of the realm I now called spiritual. As I crawled on what felt like an animal trail hollowed like a tunnel winding through the briars, I let my intuitive senses take control, dropping into a deeper state of awareness.

I never touched a thorn while following that animal trail. I was exhilarated to know I had, through intuition, discovered trails I had not been able to see. Intuition could lead me through safely when I didn't even know which direction to go other than toward the never-ending drumbeat.

Moving through shrubs and thorns, I suddenly lost focus and came out of my meditative state when distracted by the cries of fellow classmates who were not so fortunate. They had become entangled in the landscape.

"Do you still have your blindfold on?" I yelled.

"No!" hollered a desperate man.

"Put it back on," I said. "It actually helps."

The only responses were the loud sounds of crashing humans and the groans of men scratched and stabbed by thorns. Nature was letting them know who was in control.

Curious, I removed my blindfold, but all I could see were vines and shrubs intertwined like nets above and around me. I quickly retied my blindfold before fear and doubt could overtake me.

Crawling on my belly, like a snake slithering through vegetation, I pressed on.

I smelled the moss that lay like velvet over stumps in the cedar swamps. I heard the water's slow trickle as it wandered through the cedar roots and knew I was close to the creek's edge.

Once on the bank, I knew I would sink in the muck to my thighs or worse if I walked in. So, I slid into the water like a beaver, staying on my belly and paddling my way upstream in the gentle current. All the while I followed the heartbeat of the drum. When I reached the dock and removed my blindfold, the drummer signaled for me to remain quiet. unlike many of my classmates, I wore no battle scars or scratches, and the journey was amazing. I felt I had developed a new sense beyond anything I ever knew existed.

The next morning, it was obvious who had kept their blindfolds on. The students who didn't achieve that meditative state and removed their blindfolds were cut up and scratched from head to toe. Oddly, more men had struggled than women. I wondered if it was because they were trying to man through instead of tapping into the spiritual realm.

We spent the day making weapons used for hunting. We crafted rabbit sticks, bolas, and slingshots. At first, we practiced using them until we mastered the technique. Then we had to use these tools blindfolded. I had to rely on other instincts, and it shocked me how much more accurate I was than when I could see.

That night at dinner, not only did we eat blindfolded, but we also had to serve our food without seeing. I was starting to get the hang of doing things blindfolded, but the situation still challenged me. When I finally sat to eat, the food tasted different. I could detect all the ingredients.

The rest of the week was spent fine-tuning our new skills. By the last day, I felt more confident and was eager for additional training. I found it hard to say goodbye to my new friends, but we were hopeful we would see each other in future courses. It was also challenging to head home to Indiana when my heart was beginning to yearn for Colorado.

"Learning to use your intuition is one of the most important tools you will have in any situation," Dave said during our last lecture. "This will be crucial if you take the philosophy courses."

I was already signed up. The philosophy courses started right after the holidays in January. It was now September. Fortunately, some of the instructors had gathered and designed a four-day course in November on brain tanning along with an atlatl workshop.

I not only signed up, but I also registered Aunt Betsy, since Scott wasn't available, and she had expressed interest. I could only imagine the trouble Betsy and I could get into by taking the class together.

I told Betsy about signing us up for the next course.

She rubbed her hands together. "I can hardly wait. Should we practice?"

"I don't know how to do anything we'll be learning," I said.

"What should we do during the six weeks before it starts?"

"We can do a little research," I suggested, even though I'm the type of person who learns best by doing the project rather than reading about it.

We did some research, but advanced brain tanning and atlatl making seemed too complicated without guidance. We decided to wait for class before attempting either project.

This was going to be fun.

Chapter 18

Now!

IN THE SIX WEEKS BETWEEN CLASSES, Scott and I were busy setting up our new pizza franchise. It was hard for me to function in the fast-paced business world after being immersed in the flowing rhythm of the Pine Barrens. Our hometown of Granger, Indiana, seemed like an entirely different world. I longed for Colorado. Positive things had happened there, and Scott and I seemed to have negative experiences everywhere else we lived.

I wasn't feeling optimistic about the franchise either. It was the first time Scott and I were not leading together because of legalities. Scott started binge drinking, which made me concerned, because alcohol addiction ran in his family. I talked to Scott about my dream of living in Colorado, but he was too focused on the new franchise to pay much attention. To avoid depression, I focused on my next trip with Aunt Betsy to the farm. Scott hoped to join us after the business was up and running.

New Jersey Farm, November 1990

Betsy and I left Indiana at 3:00 a.m. and drove straight through until we arrived at the farm in New Jersey, where I had taken my first course. We parked in the dirt lot, grabbed our gear, and walked the long driveway to the barn.

On our way, Dave drove up in his big Hummer and gunned it in front of us.

Betsy's eyes grew wide. "Okaaaaaay."

I just smiled, knowing by her unusual silence that she felt as nervous as I was the first time. We dropped off our gear in the barn loft then joined the others below.

I didn't recognize any of the students. We were among the last to arrive, so we sat near the back. I counted five women and fifteen men. I was glad Betsy had come along.

"This class will be hands on, and there is lots to do," Derek, our instructor said, "So let's dig right in."

We worked as a team on three hides to string and stretch them around large frames made of 2x4 pieces of lumber. Then we scraped off the hair using sharp hatchets. The task was slow and tedious. We all took turns scraping the hides, which took several hours.

In the meantime, Derek gave a talk about how atlatls are used to launch the spears. It is a weapon used for hunting that predates the bow and arrow. Aborigines in Australia still use it for hunting. The atlatl is used as a launcher for the spear. Most of the guys had brought their own store-bought or precision throwers and spears. The women had nothing. We were given no training on how to make an atlatl, but after looking at the ones the guys brought, I thought Betsy and I could pull it off.

While we were waiting for our turn to scrape the hide, Betsy and I searched the property for something we could use as a spear. Next to the barn stood straight weeds about seven or eight feet tall. The weeds were already dead, so I broke the stalk at the base. The diameter was about the size of my thumb, and the center was pithy.

"Let's use these weeds for our spears," I told Betsy. "I think they'll work."

Betsy followed my lead as I removed all the little branches from the stalk. Then, I carved an arrowhead from a piece of a dead branch. I was glad to own a decent carving knife, not like the first time when I used a wimpy little fold-up job. I stuck the arrowhead in the pith of the stock and used pine pitch to hold it in place.

Betsy did the same right along with me. Since we didn't have any feathers, we gathered pine needles and lashed them on the other end with artificial sinew to act as fletching.

The finished spear was primitive and light, but it looked like it would work.

"This is cool," Betsy said. "What do we do next?"

I took the main part of the leftover branch and cut off a piece eighteen inches long and an inch in diameter. After splitting the stick in half, I kept one side and gave Betsy the other half. The wood was soft enough to take off big chunks at a time. We carved a nice flat surface on one side, leaving a bump near the bottom. Then we carved a peg and stuck it into the bump using the sinew to reinforce the entire launch area.

Betsy smiled.

I loved having someone to share this experience with. Betsy was very creative and resourceful.

"It's time to heat up the brains!" Derek yelled.

I couldn't believe it. It wasn't even noon yet, and we had finished scraping the hides and gathered our spears.

Betsy and I hurried to where the hot plates had been set up in the barn. Since no deer brains were available, we used pig brains bought at the grocery store. We heated the brains in a large soup pan. I expected them to smell rank, but they actually smelled more like boiled beef.

Once the brains were warmed, we each took a handful with our bare hands and rubbed them on the hides. It wasn't as bad as I expected. The brains weren't slimy. They were more like lumpy warm hand lotion. They made our chapped hands feel good.

Next, we took the hides off the frames and placed them in the pan with the remaining brains to soak for several hours. I was surprised. An average large soup pan can hold two deer hides. When they are wet and all scraped clean, they are thin and pliable.

While this was going on, we gathered plenty of wood for the smoker so it would put off plenty of smoke. After lunch, we draped the hides over racks in the smoker and left them to cure overnight.

The rest of the day was spent practicing throwing our atlatl spears. Many of the men's fancy ones looked perfect in every way. The guys joked about our homemade equipment, but that didn't deter Betsy and me from entering the competition that would take place the next day. The three other gals cheered as we practiced.

For dinner, we were treated to a variety of wild game. I ate elk jerky and moose sausage. Betsy went for deer and bear meat. Hers was greasy with a strong gamey taste, but mine was surprisingly good. With bellies full, we decided to call it a night.

The course ended at noon the next day, with the morning dedicated to the atlatl contest. We woke to the sound of howling wind with gusts of twenty to thirty miles an hour. That didn't stop the contest.

Our target—a picture of a deer strapped to hay bales—was about fifty feet away. Each contestant was given three tries. Whoever struck closest to the deer's heart would win.

Twelve of us entered, and Betsy and I were the only females. On our first try, both Betsy's and my spears flew end over end and sideways in the wind.

The guys laughed loud and long while the women yelled encouraging words.

I heard a voice inside me say, "Go get a flat thin rock and tie it near the bottom of the spear."

I found the perfect stone and lashed it on with some sinew.

Several guys walked by and told me that would never work, because it wasn't aerodynamic.

"It's okay," I said. "I've got an idea."

But they continued to try to convince me it wouldn't work.

On my second turn, the spear didn't blow end over end, but it still blew to the side of the target about forty-five degrees. Betsy's spear, with no weight, had the same disastrous results as our first try.

I stood watching the men throw their perfect-looking spears right into the target, but no one had hit the heart.

I was up next for my final turn. Suddenly, a gut feeling led me to face the barn instead of the target. The target faced north, and the barn was east.

The guys mumbled in the background. "What is she doing? Is she crazy?"

I closed my eyes and waited. The wind came in waves. I listened for my intuition to guide me. The wind picked up and, at the peak of the gust, I heard in my mind, "*Now!*"

I launched the dart straight at the barn. It arched up toward the roof, then gravity and the force of the wind kicked in. The gust pushed it sideways toward the target, and the rock caused the point to angle down. The spear picked up speed and thrust itself right into the deer's heart.

Betsy and I screamed and grabbed each other, jumping up and down. The other women joined us in the celebration. The look on the guys' faces was priceless. They could hardly believe what they had just witnessed.

I had won the atlatl contest.

The five of us gals ran to the target and had the guys take our picture.

Victory had never tasted so sweet. I had defied the odds, using my awareness and inner vision. I hadn't let anyone talk me out of what I knew in my gut. I had listened to the guidance, and it paid off big time.

I claimed my prize, which was a turtle shell the size of a dinner plate. Then, we packed for the trip home.

On the way out to the highway, the ladies all stopped at Burger King to clean up. We were horrified when we faced the mirror. Dirt streaked our faces. We looked as if we had just come out of the backcountry, which we had. With no mirrors at camp, we had no idea how we looked.

Then, I pointed at Betsy and laughed. "You got pig brains stuck to your hair!"

Women began grabbing their children and leaving the bathroom, giving us a wide berth. The restroom emptied quickly, leaving the five of us laughing hysterically.

Betsy and I talked the whole way home about how much fun we had. The intuition or inner vision I used during the atlatl competition had her asking questions.

"How did you know to turn forty-five degrees and face the barn? And you closed your eyes. How did you know to tie the rock on? I want to experience that."

"I learned some of these things in the other classes. It's called inner vision."

"I need that," she said.

"Okay. I'll sign you up."

I thought about Betsy's questions. Where had the voice come from? Was it a part of me? Or was it something beyond? Was it something like in my near-death experience?

I couldn't wait to find out more.

Chapter 19

The Gift

IN THE COLD MONTH OF JANUARY, I returned to the farm for the philosophy class, which was what I had been waiting for since the end of my first wilderness survival class.

The classroom was warmed by a wood-burning stove in the middle of the room. It reminded me of winters growing up at home when all we used for heat was a wood stove. Despite the rustic setting in the large red barn used for the other courses, everything was quite warm and cozy.

The longer Dave talked, the more I listened with tunnel vision, focusing straight ahead. I started to block out all the other students. It was as if Dave talked directly to me, and the words reached deep into my soul. He explained about body control and how we would do exercises to lower and raise our body temperature. He taught us about a secret place in our mind where we could go that was comfortable and safe. I imagined a big pine tree I could sit against on a canyon rim overlooking the desert valley.

I was intrigued, and my mind tried to find some logic in it all. I had never taken a philosophy class set in nature. It didn't even come close to the philosophy classes I had taken in college. Those classes had emphasized theories and long, academic words I never really understood. It was all book theories, with no applied knowledge. Here, we were applying knowledge to everything we did.

Dave said something that made me sit up straight. "Some of you may not even know this yet," he said, "but you will be teachers someday."

As soon as the words left his mouth, I knew he was talking about me. A teacher had been one of the last things I ever thought about becoming. While the thought caught me by surprise, I realized I wouldn't be a schoolteacher in the traditional sense. So, what kind of teacher would I be?

Again, I had more questions than before and still no solid answers. I spent the rest of the evening journaling before bedtime.

We spent the next few days making drums and rattles while Dave discussed various philosophies on spirituality and the history surrounding them. I found it very meditative and soothing to make these primitive items. I was reliving part of the past and felt connected to my ancestors. These tasks helped me become relaxed and prepared for the second part of the week that centered around inner vision, body control, and how the mind works.

One of the first things we worked on was body control. Our approach was that the mind and body worked together in a controlled, relaxed state to achieve the desired result. For example, the first exercise involved controlling our heartbeats. I practiced slowing my heart rate then speeding it up. We achieved this through guided meditations. Slowing it down wasn't bad, but speeding up my heart rate made me feel anxious and took me out of my calm state of mind. I was ready to move on to our next task of controlling our body temperatures.

We tried to stay warm despite the cold outside by imagining being on a warm, tropical beach. The power of my imagination changed my body temperature. Seeing how our imaginations could change things amazed me. This would be a very useful ability because hypothermia is a common killer of people who become lost in nature.

Frances, my classmate from Canada, and I decided to get up early, go down to the river, and bathe in the ice-cold water, using the principles we had just learned to stay warm. We were told to take baby steps, but I tend to stretch boundaries if the calculated risks seem reasonable.

Frances and I hardly noticed the cold as we skipped down the trail to the river. By the time we had arrived at the riverbank, the sun had just started to rise. We quickly went through our deep relaxation breathing exercises for body control and entered the water. We waded up to our thighs, and everything seemed fine, so we decided to go a little deeper, up to our waists. Then we dipped under the water.

So far, so good. We both still felt in control, so we lathered up, including our hair. Then, without warning, my legs went numb. I could barely move. I was up to my waist in the middle of the river and managed to get close to shore when I realized soap still covered my upper body and head. The water in my hair froze, and my body started to shut down from hypothermia.

"I can do this," I told myself, but I was having trouble staying focused.

"I don't think I can make it back safely!" Frances yelled.

I turned and looked at her.

She was on the other side of the river.

I didn't know how to reach her, considering I could barely move my legs. I waded a third of the way in her direction with the water up to my knees, but I couldn't safely make it any farther. I splashed my body to rinse the soap off and kept my eyes on Frances.

She was working her way toward me.

I stood there and waved her on. "You can do it!" I kept yelling. Then I realized my hair was still full of soap.

I bent over and submerged my head. It felt like it was going to explode.

Frances finally reached me, and together we made it back to shore. We were relieved, but not excited, as we were still in trouble.

Our hands, arms, and legs refused to obey our commands to move quickly. We resembled slow-motion robots, barely able to move.

We dressed without drying off and headed for the classroom. The distance to the barn was not very far, but it seemed like a hundred miles because our legs refused to hurry. Then, by the time we were two-thirds of the way, our legs started to warm up. Our pace quickened.

We nearly passed out with delight when we reached the classroom. Someone had started the wood-burning stove. We pulled up chairs as close as we could and sat waiting for our bodies to recover. My hair was still frozen in chunks.

The other students couldn't believe we had jumped in the river. "You could have died," they said, as I thawed my hair in front of the stove.

When Dave found out what we did, he half smiled at us as if he was proud. He then explained how dangerous our adventure had been. He cautioned the others not to attempt the same thing until they had acquired more experience and had learned more protocols.

The next several days were spent learning how our inner vision worked. Inner vision is a form of communication that usually doesn't involve words. Knowledge comes by way of visions, dreams, symbols, signs, and a knowingness. These conversations fascinated me. I related to what the instructor said because of my experiences with the blindfold exercises and the atlatl contest.

I thought about the Voice and all the other forms of communication I had received since I was a child. I wondered if what I experienced was the same thing as inner vision. *Could it all be coming from the same source?*

We discussed how the mind works in survival situations. A positive attitude and faith are two crucial things when faced with a challenge. We were told humans have instincts that help us survive. One of the tools we used was meditation. It relaxed our minds and allowed other forms of communication to come through by entering an alpha state of mind.

One evening toward the end of the course, we did an exercise that involved experiencing what it would be like to be in the presence of The Creator. I remember lying on my back, closing my eyes, and relaxing as I listened to soothing music playing in the background. Dave's voice was soft and gentle as he led us through a guided meditation.

I saw a wall of white light in front of me. I began to walk toward the wall of light until I stood right in front of it. Then I walked through the light and felt an incredible feeling of peace and calmness.

I opened my eyes and jumped to my feet. "I've been there before!"

"When?" asked Dave.

"During a surgery," I said.

The person next to me said, "I had a similar experience when I was unconscious for several days in the hospital."

"Sounds like you both had a near-death experience," said Dave.

He also talked about entering another realm, saying that's what we had done in our near-death experiences.

Oh my goodness! I'm finally getting some answers to my questions.

The possibility of entering that other realm without dying now seemed within reach. The idea was life changing. I felt more determined than ever to finish seeking my answers and to never give up. But I still didn't know the answer to my question I so desperately wanted to know—what happens to you when you die?

I wasn't ready to take a chance on asking Dave if he knew the answer to my biggest question, not after having people think I was nuts. It seemed I had more unanswered questions now than when I had started this journey. Yet, I also felt as if I had some new places to explore.

During the week, we held numerous discussions about healing. We briefly discussed the Bible and how different ways of healing were mentioned, especially in the New Testament. This caught my attention. Could my healing have been a result of God's intervention? If so, why me? Why did I deserve healing and being in the presence of God? I wasn't even a believer.

As I was writing in my journal, contemplating everything I had just learned, I heard a voice inside say, *With knowledge comes responsibility.*

I had no idea what that meant, but along with the Voice came a sense of peace. I wouldn't learn until much later that I heard the voice of God speaking to my soul. At the time, I merely thought it was that inner voice of guidance I had come to expect. I had never thought about where it came from.

On the morning of the last day, Dave said each of us would have a gift waiting when we arrived home. They would be special gifts from The Creator and would be different for each of us. Dave knew this because he was in tune with the spiritual realm.

On the way home, I pondered what the gift might be. I was curious, but I had no idea.

I also was hoping Scott would finally agree to move to Colorado. I felt in my spirit that we were supposed to be there. The thought of the gift was entirely out of my mind by the time I arrived home, exhausted. When I walked into the house, a card waited on the table with my name on it. On the envelope, it read "Open immediately."

I opened the card. My jaw dropped, and suddenly my tiredness was completely gone.

"I'm ready to move to Colorado right now." The card was signed by Scott.

This was my gift.

Chapter 20

Danger!

Keystone, Colorado, 1991

CHOOSING A LOCATION IN COLORADO was easy. We settled in the town of Keystone near Breckenridge, where Scott and I had married. Scott's sister had talked us into eloping instead of having a big wedding. We had loved our time there in the mountains and were excited to return where both of us could be ski bums.

When we moved to Colorado, I no longer saw Betsy. We talked on the phone a few times, but I missed the one-on-one time practicing together.

Scott and I rented a little condo at nearly nine thousand feet. I could walk out my door and up a little mountain through the sagebrush and enjoy amazing views of the reservoir and ski resorts. Scott and I loved it there, and I found it hard to leave to attend the philosophy II course back east, but I wanted to see how far I could push the boundaries of my spirituality.

Philosophy II began with playing a series of games that strengthened our communication skills, which allowed our other senses—like hearing, taste, and smell—to become more awakened. By now, I had many friends from previous classes, so I no longer felt alone in my journey for answers. I teamed up with a partner and found a small rock to hold in my hand. The other person, who faced away from me, had to guess which hand held the rock.

At first, we guessed without doing anything special and recorded the results. Next, we recorded the process we used to pick one hand over the other. We recorded our thoughts and any sensations we experienced, such as gut feelings. We recorded both our right and wrong choices. For example, I would ask myself whether I had heard a sound, or whether a voice had guided me, or if I had felt some kind of sensation. Or perhaps I had experienced a particular taste in my mouth or had seen something visually. By recording every choice, I started to see how different patterns formed.

My accuracy significantly improved as I identified these other forms of communication and how they worked to guide me. I went from being about forty percent correct when doing nothing special to eighty and up to a hundred percent using my senses. What an incredible discovery!

We were doing so well the instructor increased the difficulty of the exercise.

He made the game harder by having us guess the rock's location by giving us three or four choices instead of just two. Then we progressed to hiding the rock somewhere in the room and finding it. The final challenge was hiding it outside. The stone was more difficult to find, but we came surprisingly close in a short period of time. I was amazed at how accurate I could be with just a little practice.

Something else unexpected happened. I became more aware of the Voice that often spoke to me, and I realized it guided me in the decision-making process. Up to this point, everything I experienced had been positive and pleasant and had helped build my confidence. The first time something negative happened, it startled me.

I became uncomfortable during a simple meditation, where I began to mind travel underground to find some kind of message or hidden treasure. Something didn't feel right. Dark tunnels snaked in every direction, and roots grew out of the dirt walls. I began to crawl through the maze of roots. Out of the corner of my eye, I saw small, hideous creatures. They were staring at me, and I knew they wanted to get to me.

I looked for a way out. Too many tangled roots kept me from running, so I grabbed a root and climbed straight up into the top of what I thought was a tree. Once I reached the earth's surface, I stopped.

Prisms of sparkling crystallized light spilled around me. I basked in wonder as all fear fell away. The radiance reminded me of a magical cave from a fairy tale, with every color imaginable drawing me in; yet everything seemed so real. The contrast between this sparkling world at the top of the tree compared to the hideous underground was stunning. I could have stayed at the top forever, just like in my vision from my near-death experience, but it was not to be.

I suddenly awoke. I inhaled a couple of deep breaths before realizing it had just been a dream resulting from the meditation.

Dave instructed us to take a ten-minute break. I was glad for the breather because there was so much to process, and everything had seemed so real.

The second time, when I went into a dream-like state, I tried to go underground slowly, layer by layer. Before I knew it, I found myself slipping down what seemed like many miles of earth. I finally came to a pocket and stopped. All around me, the earth moved like liquid rock similar to molten lava in every shade imaginable.

In the center of all this, a huge eye appeared, looking straight at me. Normally, I would have been terrified, but instead, I was calm and curious.

When I looked over the ledge, a vast vortex spun right below me. It looked like the same vortex I was exposed to the week I went to hell. I don't know why I did what I did next. With the big brown eye still staring at me, I spread my arms. Then, as I let myself fall backward into the vortex, I felt it sucking me down.

"Stop!" Someone yelled.

The Voice was so abrupt and jolting that I grabbed a branch sticking out of the side of the vortex. The action broke my fall.

Who had spoken?

I couldn't see anyone, and I was still determined to discover what lay at the bottom of the vortex. I was just about ready to let go, when the Voice spoke again.

"No!"

At that moment, I knew: if I let go, I would be in serious trouble.

I was quickly learning that playing in the spirit realm, especially underground, was not a game. Instinctively, I knew the Voice I heard telling me not to let go came from God.

"He-e-e-elp!" I screamed while clinging to the branch.

Then I spotted a cave just a few yards above. I climbed the branch, one hand over the other, while the vortex increased its force, trying to suck me down.

When I finally made it to the entrance of the cave, I just stood there, lost. I wasn't supposed to be there.

Since my gut feeling kept telling me I didn't belong there, I decided the cave must be the way out. I took one step toward the entrance.

"Stop!" A voice yelled.

Suddenly, I slammed back into my body, lying on a wooden platform, shaking uncontrollably. I was tired. My eyes and stomach hurt, my heart was pounding, and I gasped for air. I thought I was going to die.

I felt like I had been to hell and back, and I wanted no more. Nothing good seemed to come from these vortexes, and now I was terrified of them.

This underground stuff is hell, and that is not a place I want to explore.

When I opened my eyes, Dave sat there staring at me. When I told him what happened, he gave me a chilling half-smile. I know now, but I did not know then, that Dave was messing around with the wrong spirits. I wanted nothing to do with that evil.

But what about all the other visions, dreams, and experiences that were so beautiful? Where did they come from?

The spiritual classes always stirred up my dreams, making them especially vivid. That night, I dreamed about a man who chose evil ways over good. I stood in the corner of a dark, dirty cellar looking around, when I started to smell something burning. I noticed a narrow tunnel and cautiously walked down it, keeping close to the walls. The smell became stronger as I moved through the hall toward another small room. It had a tiny window with bars over it, and the only light came from torches. I gagged as the odor of putrid, rotting flesh filled the air.

I peered around the corner. A man was doing a repulsive satanic ritual on a stone slab.

I could hardly breathe. An evil presence filled the place, and it made me sick to my stomach. I wanted to run, but where? So, I stood motionless.

More people entered the cellar, and I wanted to wake up from this nightmare. But how? Then suddenly, I was back in my sleeping bag. I opened my eyes and saw the barn's rafters above me and inhaled the sweet aroma of hay. Myriad sounds of the night forest calmed me. Once I realized I was safe from the nightmare, I fell back asleep.

The following day, the class was over, and we had a week off before philosophy III would begin. We were free to stay, but I decided to leave for some much-needed rest and enjoy my new Colorado home.

I was exhausted from all the visions and nightmares, but the dreams did not stop. The second evening after returning home, I had a realistic and vivid dream. I was suspended in air, looking at an enormous rock formation in a large cave. A man was walking across the ledge about forty feet high. Suddenly, the rock gave way, and the man fell. I watched in horror as falling rocks crushed his body. I smelled the dust and heard the tumbling rocks echoing through the cave. It was so real.

I woke trembling.

I shook the dream off and went back to sleep, but the nightmare returned. I tried to wake, but I was trapped in the same event. This time, the events were more intense. I couldn't see the face of the man walking on the ledge, but when the rocks broke away and fell, he went down with them. I heard all the bones in his body being crushed, and I knew he didn't survive.

After the debris settled, a rescue team tried to dig him out of the rubble. I watched with sadness at the futile rescue attempt. They weren't going to find him alive. The then a large head emerged from the rubble of rocks. The head slowly rotated toward me until I could see the face. Horrified, I recognized one of my friends I had met in Dave's class.

I woke and wanted to call my friend to warn him, but it was four in the morning. *I'll do it first thing when I get up.*

When I woke, I forgot about making the call. Later, the phone rang while I was cooking breakfast, which reminded me to call my friend. I put it off, thinking I would call him after I finished breakfast. Once again, I forgot and started my daily routines.

While I was cleaning, I came across an item that reminded me of the class. *My friend! I must call right now!*

I picked up my phone but realized I didn't have the notebook with all my classmates' numbers. It took me about fifteen minutes of looking and not finding before I was again sidetracked. It was now afternoon, and I had started to talk myself into believing the dream didn't really mean anything. Besides, what if my friend thought I was weird or just plain crazy?

As the afternoon wore on, I justified why I wasn't going to call. The more I tried to forget the whole ordeal, the less peace I felt. But I couldn't find the notebook with the phone numbers. I turned in frustration to walk across the living room I had just cleaned, when I tripped over the notebook.

The notebook was lying by itself in the middle of the room, wide open. How could that be possible?

I had just cleaned the room, and it wasn't there. If that wasn't strange enough, as I reached down to pick up the notebook, there, in huge handwriting, was the classmate's name and phone number. I couldn't argue with that kind of fate. I made the call.

He was just walking out the door to go to work. One more minute, and I would have missed him. I told him the entire story of the dream. He promised to be careful.

When I put down the phone, I felt instant relief and was at peace again.

The next morning, my friend called, excited. When I had called last night, he hadn't taken the warning very seriously and had forgotten it by the time he arrived at work. He worked the night shift in a big mine in California. That particular night, he had to walk along miles of pipeline that rested on a tall rock ledge while he checked for leaks.

As he walked, he came across the area I had described to him in detail. He stopped and stared at the cliff. "I was utterly amazed," he told me.

"What did you do?"

"I decided to climb down off the ledge and walk around the area you had described instead of walking across it."

"What would have happened if you had walked out on the cliff?"

"The pipes leak, and chemicals get down all the cracks in the rocks and dissolve them, causing rockslides," he explained. "If weight is added, they shift. If you hadn't called and warned me, I would have walked out on that ledge, and the rocks would have given way." He took a deep breath. "I could have been crushed."

We both rejoiced in the warning and the way it was given. At the time, we thought we had gained something really amazing from Dave's classes. We thought we could expect this kind of communication on a daily basis.

I would learn much later that God had given me a prophetic gift that had nothing to do with Dave's teaching. Yet, at the time, I was excited to take the next philosophy class after such an amazing event.

Chapter 21

Visions

Pine Barrens base camp, New Jersey, 1992

THE NEXT WEEK, philosophy III was held in the Pine Barrens. The focus of this course was all about how the Creator can communicate through nature. This appealed to me, as I enjoy being outside. I felt a special connection with plants and animals. They were comforting, especially in my younger years. So, when it came time to expand my experiences in this area, I felt at home.

During this course, Lou from Sweden and I became close friends. Alike in so many ways, we could have been sisters.

In the class, we learned many new techniques for body control, mostly centered around controlling fear and doubt. We practiced connecting with plants to determine if they were edible or poisonous. We also learned to find animals by using our spiritual eyes to see their tracks and the runs they used. We heightened our levels of awareness, and I began to feel one with nature by the end of the week.

Lou wanted to tour the West, so I invited her to ride home with me to Colorado and stay a few weeks.

We decided to study and practice the new physical and spiritual skills we had learned. We thought that a good trip through the Southwest and Mexico would be an adventure to test our skills. We would live out of my truck and camp along the way. Our goal was to explore more teachings on wilderness survival skills and, hopefully, find more answers to my many spiritual questions.

After seeing the changes in me, Scott and Betsy were excited to begin learning some of these skills for themselves. They had to start at the same level I did, so we wouldn't be able to take classes together. But we were looking forward to sharing our experiences. They were scheduled to take their first survival course back east in a few weeks, so Lou and I agreed that would be the perfect time to tour the Southwest.

We first stopped in Ojo Caliente, New Mexico, where we met a New Age spiritual man who sold rocks. He gave each of us a rock and told us why he chose them for us. He told me my rock, a clear crystal, stood for communication.

We told him we wanted to explore places the tourists didn't know about, so he sent us to Arroyo Hondo. The area featured a beautiful set of hot springs only the locals knew about. Unfortunately, because of the heavy snow runoff, the river had risen, completely covering the hot springs. The hot springs were located in a gorge where spiritual visions were common, so we decided to spend the night above the river.

We experienced no spiritual visions that night. Though disappointed, we were early in our trip, so we still had great hope.

The next morning, we left to visit Taos Pueblo since it was on the way to our next destination. We chose where to go by opening up a map and closing our eyes. Then we pointed to a spot on the page. Where our finger landed was our destination for the day. We stayed for as little or as long in one place as we felt led. The only constraint was the entire trip could only last three weeks.

That night we stopped at Elephant Butte Lake State Park, where we lay on the white sand by the water and watched an incredible display of falling stars. The next morning, we chose the Gila Cliff Dwellings National Monument.

We arrived at the park at midday. We ran up the trail and climbed a ladder to reach the dwellings. We purposely didn't pick up any literature, because we wanted to see if we could guess each room's purpose by using some of the techniques we had learned in class.

The park was about to close, so we didn't have much time to explore. Curious about Native American culture, we wanted to learn all we could about their ways. We decided to camp for the night and return in the morning.

That night, Lou and I lay on the top of my SUV and discussed what it must have been like living in the dwellings hundreds of years ago. I looked up at the stars and wondered what the Mogollon people thought about as they stared at the sky.

“Do you think they saw the same stars?” Lou asked as she pointed to a constellation.

“Probably,” I said.

“What do you think they were doing? Do you think they were sitting in their dwellings or looking up at the stars like we are?”

“Probably a little of both,” I said.

We both fell into our own thoughts. I was wondering what spiritual rituals they would have performed. I must have fallen asleep, because I was startled awake by a large animal crashing through the forest.

“What was that?” Lou said.

“I don’t know!” I sat still and listened. “Maybe a bear or an elk.”

The noise was moving away from us, so we felt safe enough. Awake now, we agreed to try a meditation. Our goal was to mind travel up the trail and into each of the rooms of the cliff dwellings. Then, in the morning, we would go to the Gila Visitor Center to pick up information and see how accurate we had been.

It didn’t take long for me to appear in one of the main rooms I had explored earlier in the day. The room was probably used for ceremonies and social gatherings. I was standing in a corner, watching what appeared to be a drumming session. A group of eight men sat in a circle, singing while looking down. An old man stood in front of the drummers to my left. Looking at him, I wondered if he was some kind of leader.

His head turned, and he looked at me. His gaze was so focused that it startled me.

I looked at the others who were still sitting in the circle. They were singing and looking down, unaware of my presence. When I looked back at the old man, he was still staring at me, but now he wore a grin on his face.

He reached out his hand and motioned for me to come. Nothing felt bad from this spirit, so I walked over and sat beside him.

With his finger, he drew a figure eight in the sand.

"What does that mean?" I asked.

"Go back and ask for more teachings." He pointed east.

East was home, and farther east was where I had been taking all the wilderness awareness courses. But the figure eight, I didn't understand. One of the possible meanings was infinity, but I wanted more clarification. I tried to ask more questions, but something snapped me out of the meditation, and I was back in my sleeping bag. It wasn't until much later that I realized my dream was about infinity and about where I would spend eternity.

The next morning, Lou and I compared notes. To our amazement, we experienced similar meditations. We both had seen the circle of singers drumming and the old man, but Lou was seated on his left and I on his right side. She was given a different message—the number seven. She also witnessed a beautiful sunrise.

After breakfast, we went to the Gila Visitor Center as planned to pick up some information. When we toured the little museum, we were shocked. The clothes were identical to what the men in our vision had worn. The instruments, tools, and rooms we visited also were identical. What were the odds of that happening?

These visions must mean something.

It seemed as if we were on some kind of treasure hunt. We decided to continue exploring different places until we had more answers.

Next, we felt led to visit the country of Mexico. Neither of us spoke Spanish, so we decided to spend only a few hours, just to say we had done it. We were young back then and felt we could do anything.

The border patrol just waved at us when we entered Mexico. This was before 9/11. The one-hundred-degree temperature in the Mexico desert quickly changed our minds, and we headed back to the border.

We were waiting in line to reenter the United States, when Lou informed me that she had no current visa or identification. Her visa had expired several months ago. To make matters worse, we read signs telling us what we couldn't bring across the border back into the United States, which included all of our fruits and meat.

As if those things weren't enough trouble, I couldn't find my driver's license. "Don't worry," I said, trying to stay hopeful.

"They didn't check us when we entered Mexico. Why would they care now?"

"Are you sure?" Lou said.

"You're totally blond, fair-skinned, and have a Swedish accent, and we look American," I assured her.

When our turn came, I expected the guards to wave us on by, as they had on the way in. Instead, the guards ordered us to pull to the side and step out of the truck. By now, our truck looked like it belonged to the Beverly Hillbillies, an old TV program from the sixties. We had strung deer meat in the back window, which was drying for jerky. Baskets of fruit and clothes and sleeping bags were piled everywhere.

The border police opened all the doors and pulled out our food. They started sorting through it, confiscating the apples and meat. We begged them to let us keep the food. We didn't have enough money to replace them and buy gas for the rest of the trip.

The patrol officer just stared at us as he took our bag of apples and lunch meat. He began poking things in the back of the truck with a pole, probably to check if we had any stowaways. He started to look under the passenger seat.

My stomach sank. I had forgotten about the prickly pear cactus pad we had wrapped in grass and placed under the seat for safekeeping.

“Aha!” he said, as if he had caught us in the act of some terrible crime.

I don’t blame him for being suspicious. We did look pretty rough and rather poorly groomed. We had been camping and only bathing in streams and lakes along the way. To top it off, Lou was dressed in brain-tanned leather shorts, a vest, and moccasins she had made herself.

“We are on a spiritual trip,” I tried to explain.

The guard stopped me. “Do you know that carrying grasses across the border is illegal?”

I shook my head. “No, sir, I did not.”

He whipped back around, plunged his hand under the seat, and grabbed that clump of grass wrapped around the cactus pad.

He moved so fast I didn’t have time to warn him. I grabbed Lou, and we waited for the inevitable. You know it’s a rough day when a border patrol officer jumps out of your vehicle screaming.

After the screaming stopped, he started yelling. “You tricked me! You tricked me!” He kept repeating his accusation while clutching his damaged hand.

We are so going to jail.

“What is in this grass?” he finally asked.

“Prickly pear cactus pads,” I said.

He rolled his eyes while still clutching his hand. "Why? Why do you have cactus pads rolled up in grass under the seat?"

"So we won't get pricked."

He paused and stared hard at us. "And why? Why do you have the cactus?"

"So we can roast them over the campfire tonight," I said.

His hand was already beginning to swell and turn red. He started pulling out spines, wincing with every pluck. Through gritted teeth, he asked, "Why would anyone want to roast cactus pads on a fire?"

"So we can eat them," I said.

He motioned for another officer to help him. It looked like hundreds of spines stuck in his hand. He would need a trip to the hospital. Then, with reddened face, he barked at us, "Get out of here. Now!"

We jumped into the truck and took off. Within seconds we were back in the U.S., headed up the Arizona highway. We were later told that the guards always ask for identification and check your background once you get pulled over. Thank you, prickly pear cactus!

I couldn't wait to tell Scott and Betsy about our experience. I wondered if Scott would think it was funny. Time would tell.

The next morning, while eating what little food we had left, Lou and I decided to separate for a few days. Lou wanted to stay on the Fort Apache Indian Reservation to learn about their culture and traditions. I wanted to explore Death Valley in California. There wasn't enough time to do both, so we planned for me to pick her back up in a few days. Then, we would complete our trip through Utah together.

I drove most of the night to Death Valley. I liked the uniqueness and diversity of the desert landscape. It was remote and free from human noise, and the sound of silence was breathtaking. The intermittent gentle winds created their own form of music. It reminded me of a subtle, rhythmic hum.

The next morning on the way back to Arizona to pick up Lou, I explored several wilderness areas in Nevada. The vast amount of remote land to explore seemed endless. Lou and I planned to work our way through the Grand Canyon and into Utah. We hoped to visit several national parks in Utah, where we would be within a day's drive home to Colorado. It would be our last day.

I stopped at a friend's house for a quick visit in Nevada. Lou and I chose Rick as a point of contact if anything went wrong. We both knew Rick from our wilderness classes. Lou knew I was going to check in with him on my way back to pick her up.

Rick ran out to my truck when he saw me pull in his driveway. "Lou's in trouble! She's going to call you in a few hours."

Chapter 22

The Old Man

"THERE'S SOMETHING WRONG WITH ME." Lou's voice sounded frantic. "I need to get back to Dave's farm as soon as possible!"

I couldn't imagine what had happened or why she would need to go back to where we took our beginning courses. "Why? What's wrong?"

"I'm sick . . . I—I think," she said in a shaky voice.

"What do you mean you're sick?"

"I was participating in a ceremony on the reservation, and then things turned bizarre. I felt an evil presence. It jumped on me! People in the circle began hissing, and others were squealing like pigs. One man rolled back and forth on the ground babbling like a baby, and another one was on his knees puking. I ran as fast as I could back to my tent."

Wow! What on earth happened? "Are you all right?"

"No! I'm not all right. I was tormented with nightmares all night and felt sick to my stomach. I still feel sick."

Oh my goodness, I need to go rescue Lou. "Where are you?"

"I'm on a bus headed back to the farm. We just made a stop to pick up more people, and I only have a few minutes to talk."

"Why the farm?"

"I didn't know what to do. I tried to call you, but Rick said you hadn't arrived yet, so I called the farm. They told me I was in trouble and needed to get back to them."

Lou began to cry. I felt helpless on the other end of the line, not knowing what to say.

After a moment, she whispered through tears, "They said something about possibly being possessed by evil spirits."

I thought about my experience with dreams and visions of hideous creatures that had left me exhausted and frightened. "Don't worry," I told Lou. "You're away from them now. You'll be okay."

I didn't know it at the time, but that was far from being true.

"But that's not all," Lou said. "When I got on the bus, I looked at a little girl and smiled at her. Then she screamed like she saw a devil. No one will even sit by me. It's freaking me out!"

I didn't know what to say, so I told her to keep me updated when she returned to the farm.

Once I hung up, I wasn't sure what to do. Lou and I had planned this trip together. I didn't have money, so I needed to either camp or stay with friends. I decided to call Bill and Kathy, whom I had met in one of my previous classes. Perhaps I could meet up with them. They lived in nearby Utah.

"Sure," Kathy said. "We would love to have you. We'll go camping in the Uinta-Wasatch-Cache National Forest.

That night, while I slept in my tent to the sweet aroma of ponderosa pine, I had a vivid dream. Soon, it bordered on a nightmare. In the dream, I saw familiar faces of spirit guides and people I had thought were good. They were laughing and smiling, but when I ran up to them, they turned into hideous beings. Each time, I would run for my life, hearing them cackling like witches behind me.

Just when I thought the whole ordeal was over, I would come across another scene with a group of people I recognized as good people—even friends. Yet, once I approached them, the same thing happened as before. They suddenly morphed into some kind of monster, or evil person, and chased me, cackling all the way. This went on for what seemed like hours. Exhausted because it all seemed so real, I couldn't wake no matter how hard I tried.

Finally, one of the people in my dream said, "You can wake up once you figure out why we're here."

"Why are you here?" I needed the truth.

They all started to laugh and change forms. But, between laughs, they gave me a clue as they mocked me. "Which ones of us are good?" they taunted. "And which ones of us are not?"

They continued to deceive me, and no matter how hard I tried, I could not tell evil from good.

"I don't know!" I yelled. I was sitting on the ground, defeated, when a familiar figure appeared out of the corner of my eye.

I recognized the old man. He was the same one, still dressed in a brown cloak, who had appeared to me weeks earlier in my vision at the Gila Cliff Dwellings. He smiled at me and motioned for me to come closer.

Cautiously approaching, I hoped the old man wouldn't shift into some hideous being, as the others had. As I moved closer, I felt a different presence about him than I had with the others. His presence felt deeply caring and loving.

I sat down across from him, feeling strangely at peace.

He began to teach me, explaining that some individuals and spirits are quite good at disguising their true identity. "The only real power they have is deception," he said. "It's very important that you learn how to discern different spirits and their motives."

"How do I do that?"

"By relying on your inner voice, a higher power, for guidance," he explained.

"I don't understand. I'm using all the tools and skills I have learned so far, but nothing seems to work like it used to."

"That's because those tools don't work. The dark side knows how to get around such things." His warm brown eyes focused on me. "And what you are discovering is dangerous if you don't know who you are."

With that, he was gone.

I woke from the dream exhausted and with more questions than answers. I had been running from those hideous creatures for what seemed like hours, and I had no idea what the old man meant by knowing who I am. And why were my tools no good?

I mulled over my questions until I finally fell asleep.

I woke the next morning feeling strangely refreshed. I joined Kathy and Bill in a day of practicing our primitive skills. By afternoon, I could barely keep my eyes open from all the hiking and practice, so I went off by myself, sat down under a pine tree, and took in all the gorgeous mountain views. Still disturbed by the nightmare, I wondered what it all meant. Worn out, I lay down and shut my eyes for a little rest. In only a few minutes, I was dreaming again.

I stood before a group of people who were staring at me intently. No one said a word, but I knew this was a test. I recognized all the faces as being spirit guides who had helped me throughout the years, but something seemed different. I wasn't as eager to just run up and give them a big hug.

One of them, a light-skinned Native American, approached, and reassured me. “It’s okay now, it’s me.”

I recognized him from previous dreams and meditations. He had always seemed friendly, but I didn’t feel the peace with him I had felt with the old man last night. None of the other spirit guides had ever given me the peace the old man had.

“I’m here to help you,” the spirit said.

I wanted to be sure who this really was. I waited for a sign, or some form of guidance about what to do next. While I waited, more spirits appeared out of the background. At first, I tried talking with them and asking questions, but all they would do was laugh, even the Native American.

I thought about what the old man had said and about how I should listen for that higher power of guidance. I had no idea, however, how to do that. All the voices sounded the same. By now, all the spirits were forming a circle around me.

I tried running away, but I couldn’t escape. Everywhere I ran, there they were.

Then I noticed the old man from the cliff dwellings, standing to the side. He pointed to his eyes. “Look into their eyes.”

I immediately turned to the group and did as he instructed, but nothing happened.

“Look *into* their eyes, not *at* their eyes,” he said. “Go deeper, past the surface, and you will see into their souls.”

Even though the creatures were still laughing and being obnoxious, like teenagers on drugs, I took a deep breath, relaxed, and went deeper. I kept going deeper until I could no longer visually see the creature's eyes. It was like looking through a forest but not seeing the trees. I was now seeing who they really were.

The spirits were all disguised to fool me. They looked good on the surface, but I now had a window into their souls. And in this place, there was no hiding the truth. They were still trying to deceive me, but it wasn't working. Within seconds of looking into their souls, I saw them all turn back into the evil, grotesque beings they had been all along.

Then a big flash of bright light filled the sky. It reminded me of my first near-death experience. I also recalled the same flash of light I had seen when I came out of my last nightmare about hell.

Immediately I awoke from the dream, staring into the startling blue sky. I realized that good things always happened after the flash.

I sat gazing into the woods, amazed at what I had discovered. I thought about people and how easy it would be for a person to look good on the surface yet be rotten on the inside. Now, I could look into their souls and know the truth.

Could such a thing really be possible? Sure, it had worked in my dream, but what about in the physical realm, with real people? *Is this why I avoid certain people I have a bad feeling about?*

Could the higher power the old man had talked about be the one alerting me to people's real intentions?

As I gathered my thoughts, I heard Kathy and Bill approaching. I rose and met them halfway. I told no one about the vision or dream, though I wondered what Scott would think. I wanted to understand it myself first.

The next morning, I packed my gear and headed home. I faced an eight-hour drive and looked forward to some possible insights on the events that had taken place during the last several weeks. Driving was an excellent place to listen to my inner vision. I wondered about Lou, but she was still on the bus making her way back to New Jersey. I would hear more from her in due time.

Chapter 23

The Maple Tree

I WAS TOO EXHAUSTED to receive any new revelations on the way home. Besides, I was still basking in the tremendous flow of insight from my dream. After this trip, I couldn't go back to my old life. The freedom I experienced during the last few weeks made me realize just how much Scott's addictions had affected me. They wore me down mentally and physically. His drinking and use of drugs were beginning to escalate.

The next day after I arrived home, Lou called. "I made it back to the farm," she said, "but I'm on a payphone and only have a couple of minutes to talk."

"Are you better?" I asked.

"I'm exhausted, but better." Lou sounded calm. "I'm going to stay here and help out for at least the next six months. I'll live in the Pine Barrens and be a caretaker at base camp."

"That's awesome. Scott and I will be back to take the advanced awareness class this fall. We can all connect again." I hoped Scott would be better by then.

"I can't wait to see you," Lou said. "I'll be stronger."

"Me too." I really wanted to ask her more, but now was not the time. She could fill in the details at our next meeting.

When Scott returned home, he was still using drugs, so I suggested we go our separate ways for a while.

Scott couldn't bear the thought of losing me. He believed our troubles were because I had become more connected to the spiritual realm. He was sure something other than his addictions were adding to our problems.

Part of his reason for taking survival classes was the hope of restoring our relationship. He had recently returned from taking the last survival class prerequisite, so he could now take some of the more advanced courses with me. He was excited that we could attend together, but our first class wouldn't happen until fall, which was still several months away.

Meanwhile, Scott had a chance to partner in a construction business with a friend, Eric, who lived in Scott's hometown of Minneapolis, Minnesota. The opportunity seemed good, and he asked me to give him another chance, so we packed up and moved.

With the help of Scott's ex-girlfriend from high school, Michelle, we rented a small house near where she and her husband lived. But Scott soon reconnected with many of his former buddies and fell back into some old drug habits. This placed more strain on our marriage. I didn't want anything to do with drugs. I loved

Scott and he was a nice guy. I hoped this was a phase he would soon get over.

We lived in the suburbs, and I was new to the area, so I started getting to know Michelle, who ended up being a real lifesaver for me. She didn't do drugs, and she was into all the survival techniques I was practicing. She was also interested in the spiritual things I was learning and never mocked me. She even lived in an old house that was a bit haunted. Since she wanted to learn more about the spiritual realm, the two of us got along well together. She introduced me to others who were interested in what I was doing.

The problem was everyone was working outside the home but me. I couldn't find a job, so my days were rather lonely. I began filling them by practicing my tracking skills. I squared off an area of dirt to be used as a tracking area. Then I used the end of a broom handle and poked holes into the dirt. I wrote in my journal what the holes looked like and included the weather, temperature, humidity, and barometric pressure. I would come back an hour later to track changes. This technique is called aging tracks. I became so good at it that I could be really accurate with the weather. I could even tell when the barometric pressure would change.

One night, Scott invited friends over and, afterward, they walked through my tracking area. The next day, I could tell within minutes when they had stepped into that area.

Despite the move, the new opportunity, and all our new friends, Scott and I continued to spiral downward in our relationship.

I hoped that taking our next class together would help mend things.

One day, I was lying on our couch staring out the sliding glass door at a huge maple in the front yard. The branches were swaying in the wind when I noticed they were leaving aura trails. I blinked my eyes, then rubbed them, but nothing removed the trails from my vision. Every branch and leaf was outlined with a light blue aura. It reminded me of the northern lights dancing in the night sky, except this was daytime.

I had heard about auras, but this was the first time I had experienced them. Something stirred deep within my spirit, like an awakening of some kind. I sensed a deeper connection to things living around me. *Is this the spirit of the tree?*

The maple's aura was so alive and rich. It seemed as if I was looking into another realm of brilliant dancing lights.

Could this be real?

The experience reminded me of when I was a child and would climb high in a large maple next to our house. The tree was one of the tallest in the area. From the top, I could see for miles. I spent hours at the top, cuddled in the forked branches. When the wind blew, the tree swayed as if I rested in a smooth gliding rocker.

Sitting so high up was like being in a different world. I started talking to the tree, telling it all my problems. I felt like the tree understood me and always tried to comfort me, especially when I was sad or crying.

Shortly after settling in, the wind would start blowing, even on calm days, and the tree would sway, rocking me back and forth. Then I would hear music and songs coming from the branches and leaves as the wind blew softly through them. It felt like the arms of someone great were wrapped around me, and God was telling me that everything was going to be all right.

I spent more and more time in the top of that big maple tree. I always faced west, seeing visions of great adventures. They were about places out West. These visions continued for years until we moved down the road to a new house. I didn't understand, at such a young age, all the future events I was being shown, but I enjoyed the different landscapes and looked forward to visiting all those places in the future. I didn't know then, but these were some of my first forms of communication from the Creator. Since then, I've visited many of those same places.

Now, as I stared at the maple tree outside the window and watched the auras swaying, I wondered about my connection with Creator.

Has he always been in my life?

The back door opened, and Scott entered the room.

"Look at the tree," I said. "Do you see them?"

"See what?"

"The auras."

He stared hard. “Where?”

“Around the tree.” The branches left amazing sweeps of color with every sway.

“I don’t see anything but a tree,” he said.

I blamed it on the drugs. Drugs can never take the place of or come close to the euphoria, love, and freedom I had experienced during my near-death experience. There’s just no substitute for the real thing.

My heart sank with the knowledge that Scott could not see what I saw, that we didn’t share this ability. Scott and I still loved each other, but the closeness we had always enjoyed was fading. We both hoped the advanced awareness class would draw us back together.

Chapter 24

Aura Trails

Pine Barrens, New Jersey, 1994

SCOTT AND I ARRIVED AT BASECAMP for the advanced awareness course on a beautiful warm fall day. The first thing I did was look for Lou.

"Sooby-Dooby-Doo!" Lou yelled from the kitchen area.

"Looby-Dooby-Doo!" I yelled back.

We embraced each other and jumped up and down while we laughed. After catching up, Lou led Scott and me down some small trails through the Pine Barrens until we came to her campsite. Since she was a caretaker and needed to be close, her site wasn't very far from base camp.

She had set up a pup tent with a lean-to next to it. Inside the lean-to were several primitive projects she was working on. She stored her clothes and other items she didn't want to get wet inside the tent. Lou pointed to a hogan from a previous class that stood a few yards behind her shelter. "That's where I sleep."

The hogan, about eight feet in diameter and four feet tall, was made of sticks and debris.

"You did a nice job fixing this shelter up," Scott said.

I pointed to the lean-to, "Look at all the cool things she's making."

"I've had a lot of time to practice." Lou held up some of the clothing made of brain-tanned leather, a beautiful pair of moccasins, and some amazing pouches. I admired other items behind her—just as beautiful—shirts, shorts, and just about anything a person could think of made from leather.

"I was able to sell some items to other students," Lou said.

"They're amazing," I said.

"I plan on using the money to head back West after class," Lou laid the clothing down.

"Where will you go?"

"I'll probably start in New Mexico. I met some people in one of the classes who invited me to stay on their compound. They like living off the land."

I was happy for Lou. It seemed things were looking up for her. I wanted to ask more, but one of the instructors whistled for everyone to return to base camp. We gathered in the kitchen area.

"Okay, everyone," Ben announced, "This class is going to involve a lot of personal time. We will not be working in groups, so I want each of you to go find a personal sit spot close to camp."

I headed to the edge of the cedar swamp while Scott chose somewhere in the pines. We were given until dinner to set up our tents and find our sit spots. After dinner, Dave gave us further instructions. "I want you to walk slowly to your sit spots," he said. "Once you get there, I want you to journal everything about your surroundings and especially take notice of wildlife." Then he dismissed us.

I walked along a trail to a small clearing in the pines. A little sandy berm edged the forest, so I sat there, facing the cedar swamp. A few other students sat nearby, but that didn't bother me, as they were quiet.

After journaling for what seemed like forever, I looked up and noticed the sun was setting. Insects started in with their orchestrated calls. A beautiful glow filled the sky, and the aroma of warm cedar washed over me. That's when it happened.

Auras formed halos around the students near me. I rubbed my eyes and blinked, but I still saw them clear as day. One student had a light green color around her head, and another had purple. I thought it was a fluke, but as more students walked by on their way back to camp, auras outlined their entire bodies. As the darkness deepened, the colors didn't fade. In fact, they grew brighter. I watched with amazement until the last student passed by.

Complete darkness had blanketed the wilderness by the time I returned to camp. Most people had already gone to bed. I chose not to say anything about what I had seen. I was tired and wanted to wait until morning to learn if anyone else had seen what I had. The experience made me wonder. I had thought the aura waving around the maple back in Minnesota had been some kind of anomaly. I could hardly wait to discover what others had experienced in their sit spots.

The next morning, I asked Scott what he had seen.

"I didn't experience anything out of the ordinary."

I told him about my experience.

"Oh! I've seen those before," he said. "I didn't know what to think of them." He explained that he had learned in his philosophy class that auras are residuals left behind from the spirit realm. "You don't usually see them unless you are intentionally looking for them."

"Weren't you intentionally looking for them in the maple tree back home?"

"I wasn't in the right state of mind," he confessed.

During breakfast, no one else seemed to have seen anything unusual, so I waited for the lecture to start.

"Okay, folks," Dave said. "This morning, we are going to practice camouflage. Two of us are going to hide along the trail to the creek. Your job is to find us. We won't be more than a few feet off trail."

Dave wanted us to give them twenty minutes to hide, so I went and found Lou.

"The wildest thing happened while I was in my sit spot last night," I said. "I saw auras."

"Were you at the cedar swamp?" Lou asked.

"Yes."

"I've seen them there too."

I wanted to ask her more, but Ben whistled for us to start looking for Dave and the other hidden instructor. All of us started walking along the trail while staring into the underbrush.

I looked in the willow thickets and behind trees.

Nothing.

After about fifteen minutes, Ben gathered us around him and told us to look in a specific direction. Out popped Dave, and to his left, the other instructor appeared.

My jaw dropped. They had only hidden two or three feet in front of us, and I had never seen them.

As they drew near, I smelled the swamp mud they used to cover themselves with patterns that looked like bark.

How could I have missed that?

We spent the rest of the morning practicing camouflage until lunch. After lunch, we learned more advanced methods of tracking on debris and other hard surfaces. Then, Dave started talking about spirit tracking.

"When an animal walks by," Dave said. "They leave a trail behind in the spirit, kind of like a spiritual footprint or residue."

My interest piqued. This is what Scott had been talking about.

Dave continued, "You can see it if you look into that realm." He paused. "Humans do the same thing." He promised that we would practice seeing spiritual footprints in a few days.

I could hardly wait. Meanwhile, we students continued to journal at our sit spots and practiced hearing concentric rings. Dave wanted to make sure we could achieve an alpha state of mind or deeper before he taught us spirit tracking.

When the day arrived, we started with meditations. Then we moved to tracking, but I detected nothing. I couldn't see any trails left behind by animals.

I was bummed, until the night tracking started.

Once it grew dark, we gathered along the road leading into base camp. We looked toward the forest, and I instantly saw them. Trails of color shot through the Pine Barrens. Some trails of color lingered in the trees, probably left by squirrels and birds. Others moved through the debris and underbrush. I couldn't tell which animal had left them, but I saw the aura trails.

Many students experienced a gut feeling or sensed where the animal trails were. Only a few actually *saw* the trails, though.

The next morning, everyone talked about their experiences at breakfast. When Dave overheard me telling some students how I could see brightly colored trails at night, he looked at me and grinned.

His response made me feel as if I had been given something special. Was my ability to see auras a gift?

On the other hand, I also was beginning to be able to discern spirits. Something didn't seem quite right, but I didn't know why.

Chapter 25

Everett

LATER THAT DAY, LOU AND I TALKED about what happened after we had separated on our trip. She told me she had found herself in an unsafe situation that involved the dark side. Because of this, she now wanted to focus on physical skills. She never wanted a repeat of that episode.

"It's safer," she said, "just learning the physical skills and a little awareness."

She had a point. Dave had talked about how the spiritual realm can mess you up, or even kill you, if you don't know what you're doing. I learned much later that it is very dangerous to mess around with things in the spirit world. Not everything is safe there, and it's important to be grounded with the right foundation. But at that time of my life, while taking the advanced awareness class, much of that realm appealed to me.

The next time we went to our sit spots, the traffic of students walking by distracted me, so I moved. I wanted to go deeper into the cedar swamp. The few times I had explored them in the past were magical.

No place on earth is like the cedar swamps. They aren't smelly and boggy like what one normally thinks of as a swamp. The water is clear and cold, like high mountain streams. The cedars weep tiny beads of sap that catch the sunlight in sparkles of color. The cedar swamps of the Pine Barrens are truly enchanting.

The cedar swamp bordered our main camp. It provided a great place to sit, because of all the water surrounding each tree and the unique ecosystem. Every tree, or sometimes a small grouping of trees, would be surrounded by clear, slow-moving water anywhere from one- to three-feet deep. The water moved toward the creek, which made its way through the forest.

In order to move deep into the swamp without getting wet or sinking in quicksand, I had to jump from tree clump to tree clump. The clumps were mostly made up of roots and moss-like vegetation. The bases of the clumps were never level, which left little room for error. In some areas, instead of hopping from tree base to tree base, I walked across fallen gumwood trees that had been cut down and left by loggers.

Soon, I was deeper than I had ever been in the swamp. Small rays of light reflected off calm waters, giving the moss a soft, cozy look like that of velvet. The aroma of cedar and fresh vegetation made my senses come alive. It was like being in an enchanted forest. The day was hot, but cold water running through and around the base of the cedars cooled the air.

I was drawn to the base of a gumwood that had been cut down. Next to it, on the same little island, stood a tall cedar tree. I sat on the gumwood stump and leaned against the cedar. I was taking in the beauty of the area when the tree trembled.

I sat up and glanced around. Seeing nothing, I leaned back against the tree. All kinds of little bugs and tadpoles swam in the clear water surrounding my island. I saw several unique frogs that only live in cedar swamps.

I was just getting relaxed, and had closed my eyes, when the cedar trembled again. This time it shook harder and lasted longer. I jumped up. Still, I saw nothing.

I sat back down and leaned against the tree. Within minutes the tree began to shake. I jumped to my feet, spun around, and stared at the tree. Then I searched all around the tree to see if any of my friends were playing a joke. I was absolutely alone.

I thought about getting out of there, but I wasn't sure what I would be running from.

"What's going on?" I said jokingly as I studied the tree.

"Are you going to hurt me?"

This is weird, I thought. Where was the voice coming from? "Who are you?" I kept searching around the tree, sure someone was playing a joke. I didn't see a single soul.

"Are you here to kill me like they killed my friend?" The voice sounded shaky and trembly, like someone about to cry.

By now, I didn't know what to think. "Who are you?" I asked again.

"Everett," the clearly male voice said. "They killed my friend."

I sprang to my feet and jumped back to the cedar and checked behind it.

No one.

"They hurt him," the voice continued. "And then he slowly started to die. Later, they came back and cut him down and left him lying beside me."

I considered the lifeless log I had been sitting on and then the stump next to the cedar. "I don't want to hurt anyone," I assured Everett. *Oh my goodness! I'm communicating with a cedar tree.*

Perhaps if I had been back in Minnesota, the exchange would have seemed even more strange. But there, in the enchanted cedar swamp and while delving deep into the spiritual realm, anything seemed possible.

Many readers will have trouble believing this, but Everett and I held quite a conversation with no drugs involved. He explained he had grown up with the gumwood tree at his side. Then, one day, someone came along and injured the gumwood. I realized a logger had ringed the tree, causing it to begin to die. Later, the logger returned and finished it off by cutting it down and leaving the main trunk behind.

Everett told me a sad story of how he was alone and scared. He deeply missed his friend, who had been cut out of his life.

As I listened to him tell his story and thinking that no one would ever believe me, I remembered my mother had said she could always hear trees screaming when they were being cut. So, maybe hearing from a tree wasn't as unusual as it seemed.

That night, around the campfire, I decided to be brave and share my experience. I was surprised to learn that Mark, a logger from the Pacific Northwest, had no problem at all believing me.

"Every time I would start to log a forest," Mark said, "trees would throw pine cones, needles, and branches at me. I would have to stop, get off my machine, and talk to the trees. If I didn't, it was disastrous. So, I always explained why I was there and what the trees would be used for and become. After I explained things, the forest would settle down."

Our stories intrigued everyone around the campfire. No one doubted I was telling the truth. We were all there to go deeper into the supernatural, and all of us had experienced it in some way or another. Their admiration and acceptance validated my experience. I no longer felt weird. I wasn't the only one who talked to trees.

I communicated with Everett in other classes, but I've never had another tree or inanimate object talk with me . . . so far.

Chapter 26

Purple Mountains

BEING IN THE ADVANCED AWARENESS CLASS with Scott was good for both of us. We were away from our busy schedules and the demands of life, and nature allowed us the opportunity to slow down and live in the moment. Yet, it did little to solve our problems. As soon as we arrived home, Scott returned to using drugs, and our relationship continued to spiral.

Living with drugs was not my choice for a path I wanted to take. We soon found it difficult to agree on any common ground. Together, we decided to part ways. We divorced but would remain friends. On an incredibly sad day, I packed my little U-Haul and said good-bye to Scott. We hugged each other, and that was it.

A part of me died that day, so I threw myself into living the adventures I had always dreamed about as a kid while sitting high in the maple tree. The visions I received helped me overcome my grief.

Since I was now homeless, I headed back to my hometown of Granger, Indiana, to stay with my brother and his family for a few weeks. I had no idea where I would end up, but I needed to regroup and save some money. With only a few hundred dollars to my name, I needed a place to store my things until I decided where I would live.

The two weeks spent with my family were humbling. When I arrived at my brother's house, a cot in his basement utility room was the only place to stay. I didn't mind, because it was warm and only temporary. The real humbling part came when I went to ask the man who had purchased our pizza business if he had a job for me.

When we owned the business, I used to ask Scott, "How do these employees survive on just one hundred dollars a week?" Now, a year and a half later, I asked for that very thing. I was once the owner and top authority figure. Now, I would be at the bottom, but I desperately needed money. The new owner was generous enough to offer me a job, so I took it.

I planned to use the money for gas to head back east for a winter survival course I had won in a contest the preceding year. Cold weather was the hardest season for me to deal with, but I wanted to spend a month in the woods to clear my mind.

Two weeks later, I had reached my goal and drove off to the survival course. I could have returned to live with my family and work a nine-to-five job. I chose, instead, to be homeless and live out of my truck. I felt such freedom going where my heart led. I spent the first week and a half at the farm in New Jersey taking an advanced primitive skills course. This week gave me time to adjust to the cold weather and allowed more time for practice.

The advanced skills class was a last-minute addition to the schedule, so enrollment remained small with about thirty students. I recognized a few people, but I didn't know them well. We worked on more intricate projects like ceremonial pipes and drum making, leather pouches, moccasins, beadwork, and baskets. We worked long hours individually on pieces, so I only connected with people on a surface level.

After the course ended, I stayed on the farm for a few days before heading to base camp in the Pine Barrens. That's when things turned interesting.

One of the instructors, Jason, had a friend whose Mom had traveled to Egypt. While there, she had purchased a necklace that had been in the tomb of a mummified Egyptian. On the plane ride home, she decided to wear the necklace. A week later, she died of some rare, aggressive cancer. The daughter thought the necklace was evil and dangerous and wanted nothing to do with it, so she had given it to Jason to destroy.

Several of us were sitting in the farmhouse's living room when one of the instructors started messing with the necklace, which was in a box. We all had heard the story and should have known better than to touch it, but two of the guys ran to see it.

I was terrified and jumped behind the couch. Another gal joined me.

"Don't let anyone touch it!" Jason yelled.

Jason soon got everything under control, but the one student who had looked at the necklace began experiencing horrible nightmares. This same student, months earlier, had visited a museum where they exhibited mummies. The display was roped off for repairs, but a coffin remained. He went over and climbed in to see what it felt like. I don't know how long he laid there, but afterward, the worst gut-wrenching nightmares plagued him for several months. Now, after staring at the necklace, the nightmares were back with a vengeance.

That one experience was enough for me. I didn't want anything to do with Egypt and mummies.

I packed up and headed to base camp in the Pine Barrens the next day. Several of us camped there until the winter survival course started. I spent the week helping build a temporary shelter for lectures. During this time, I became acclimated to the cold and relaxed into a deeper state of awareness. I felt nervous about this winter survival class, but it turned out to be one of my favorite courses.

We worked in teams of six people, which made things a lot more manageable and fun and took my mind off my troubles with Scott. We built a shelter that we lived in for almost two weeks as a group. We sat in our shelters at night with a little fire in the center and worked on projects like our ancestors did hundreds of years ago. We made bows, arrows, baskets, clothing, and straw mats that would be used for sleeping bags. We also worked on awareness skills. Body control seemed much easier than previous attempts years ago when I had tried to bathe in the river during freezing temperatures. Acclimating to cold weather several weeks before the course turned out to be a huge benefit.

One morning, three of us washed our hair and bathed in the creek while the temperature hovered at zero degrees. We didn't dillydally, but we cleaned up without freezing to death. The hardest part was rinsing all the soap out of my hair before it froze. We did have to thaw our hair by the fire before we could comb it. I couldn't believe I had adjusted so well to the cold weather.

After living out in the woods for a little more than a month, the time came to move on, but I hadn't given my living conditions much thought. I decided to follow my heart and ask Creator to lead me to my next destination. Dave had mentioned Creator in earlier classes, and I was sure that was the Voice I had been hearing. I felt a strong calling to head west, so that's what I did.

During the next three months, I had no place to call home other than my truck, which the bank probably wanted back since I couldn't make payments. I headed to Nevada. The drive was uneventful until I arrived in the desert of Arizona close to sunset.

Vivid colors filled the sky with reds, pinks, oranges, and purples of every shade. I pulled to the side of the road and stared at the mountains in the distance. I had heard about the purple mountains through songs, but now they filled the sky with the deepest, most brilliant shades of purple I had ever seen in nature. I captured the moment in my mind as the fading rays of light left the sky. Then I pulled back on the road and headed west.

On my entire drive to Nevada, I constantly prayed for guidance and direction, keeping my mind on what was ahead instead of what was behind. I didn't even listen to music. I drove enveloped in silence while listening for that still, small voice of instruction.

I only heard from Scott one time. While driving through the Midwest, I had stopped at my parent's house. They told me he was trying to get in touch, so I called to see what he wanted.

"The bank wants to know where you are," Scott said. "They want to repossess the truck."

"Don't tell them," I said. "I'll work it out."

I had no idea how I was going to pay.

Incredible night views replaced the brilliant purples as I continued west. It was like I was driving in a planetarium. Stars filled the sky in every direction.

Before long, another glow appeared on the horizon. That glow could only be one thing, Las Vegas, Nevada. As I neared the city, it reminded me of a Fourth of July celebration. I saw one big light display, which seemed like a world of its own. The intense energy of the city shocked my senses, so I drove straight through and headed for Boulder City to stay with friends.

Tired of my nomadic ways, I wanted to settle down. But so far, no place felt right. Still, I believed Creator would lead me. I was down to my last twenty-five dollars, but I clung to faith that an answer would come soon.

Chapter 27

The Miracle

TWO DAYS LATER, while still in Boulder City, I was counting what little money I had when the phone rang. My friends were away at work, so I answered, which was unusual, because I had never answered someone's phone before.

"Hello."

"Sue?" said a surprised voice.

"Who is this?"

"It's me, Michele."

I couldn't believe it. "How did you find me?"

"You gave me this number a while back as a possibility of someone who could find you if I needed to get in touch. And I need to get in touch with you. But I never expected you to answer the phone."

"I can't believe you found me," I said. "Is everything okay?"

"No! Everything is not okay. You need to come back here. Now!"

I was still recovering from answering someone else's phone and the call actually being for me. Had someone died? What could possibly be so important? "What's wrong?"

"It's Scott," Michele said. "I can't explain it all on the phone."

"Is he okay?"

"Yes. No. Well, he's okay physically, but something is wrong. He's seeing my friend."

Wow, he moved on fast. To Michele, I said, "He can see whoever he wants. We're divorced."

"But something isn't right," she said. "Something is very wrong."

I knew from past experience that Michele was in tune with the spiritual world. If she thought something was wrong, then it probably was.

"You just have to come back right away," she said.

At that suggestion, I thought she had lost her mind. I had no money. It's not like traveling clear across the country was an easy jaunt. Besides, I had just arrived here. "That's not possible," I said. "I'm in Nevada with only twenty-five dollars left to my name." I paused for a moment, thinking about the many times I had counted the twenty-five dollars during the last few days hoping it would somehow grow.

"It doesn't matter," Michele insisted. "You have to come back. I will lend you the money."

Deep inside, I felt she was right. I had been feeling a tug to go back to Minnesota since yesterday. I had tried to ignore it because—no matter how many times I counted—I only had twenty-five dollars left, and that certainly wouldn't take me across the country. Now, with Michele finding me out of the blue, I knew I had to go back. But how?

"I'll call you back when I figure things out," I said.

She wanted to wire money, but this was back in the day when we had to use Western Union. To make matters worse, it was already late afternoon, which meant places would be closed by the time I arrived at the next major city with a Western Union. I thought about waiting another day, but my gut told me to leave immediately.

I was studying my map, trying to figure things out, when a Voice inside my head said, *"Open your wallet and count your money again."*

I had counted it multiple times during the last few weeks and searched everywhere for extra money but had found nothing. I knew exactly what was in my wallet.

The voice was persistent, *"Count your money again."*

So, I pulled out my wallet and began to count the same one-dollar bills again.

When I reached the last crumpled bill, I noticed some crisp new bills that had not been there before. I just stared at them. Five brand new twenty-dollar bills—the exact amount I needed to return to Minnesota.

I immediately called Michele. "You will not believe what just happened." I had no idea where this money had come from, but I knew it was an answer to prayer, and I told her so. "I'll be home soon."

I wrote a short note to the friends I was staying with, thanking them for all they had done. I was packed and heading northeast toward Salt Lake City within five minutes. I had no idea what awaited me, but I felt sure I was doing the right thing.

I drove straight through, stopping only once for a two-hour nap. I should have been completely exhausted when I arrived in Minnesota, but I was far from tired. Stars filled the sky on the moonless night when I arrived at Michele's house.

"I'm so glad you're here," Michele said, inviting me in. Then she explained, "I had a dream, and I was told to find you and tell you to come back. It haunted me all day, and I have had no peace until I talked with you and convinced you. I still won't have total peace until you go talk to Scott."

"I've only talked to him once in three months," I pleaded. "I can't just show up at his house."

She grabbed me by the arms and begged. "Please."

I picked up the phone and called Scott to see if he was home.

No answer.

I felt unsettled in my stomach. I closed my eyes and asked, "What do I do now?"

A soft, clear voice said, *"Go over to his house."*

"But he's not home."

"Trust me."

I had learned by now that I really could trust this inner voice. I said goodbye to Michele, jumped in my truck, and drove straight to Scott's. I parked on the street. Lights shone in his house, which made me hopeful, but I knew he had a roommate, so I still wasn't sure. I walked up the little hill that led to the front deck. Once on the deck, I peered through the sliding glass doors. Dim light illuminated the living room, with brighter lights coming from the kitchen. I pressed close to the glass door for a closer look inside. I didn't see anyone.

"Hello!" I said. "Is anyone home?"

I saw movement in the kitchen area and began to tap on the sliding glass door while still yelling, "Hello."

A minute later, Scott walked into the living room while talking on the phone.

I stood there with a big smile on my face, waving at him.

His eyes widened, and his jaw dropped as he hung up the phone. He opened the door and stared. "What are you doing here?"

It felt really strange to be standing on his porch like that. "Michele called me while I was out in Nevada," I said. "She said I had to come back. She said it had something to do with your new girlfriend and that it wasn't right."

He began to laugh out loud.

Not the reaction I had expected. "What's so funny?"

He invited me in and explained that the girlfriend in question had been sitting in the beanbag chair, facing the patio doors, when the phone rang. He had gone into the kitchen to find some information for a friend when he heard his girlfriend call out. He turned to see what the problem was.

She pointed toward the sliding glass doors with a shocked expression on her face.

He looked but didn't see anything.

"Is-isn't that your ex-wife?"

He looked again, but before he could say a word, his girlfriend jumped up and screamed.

"It's her! It's Sue!" She yelled.

Scott was still trying to figure out how I could possibly be standing outside his patio doors when he knew I was somewhere out West.

"Oh my God!" the girlfriend said. "It's a sign. You two are supposed to be together." Then she ran out the back door.

He ran after her and tried to explain he didn't have any idea what was happening, but she refused to reason with him. She told him we were meant to be together, and they must never see each other again.

Meanwhile, I had no clue all this was going on in the backyard while I was on the front deck. I felt like I was in some kind of twilight zone, and I knew I was supposed to be there at that very moment. "I'm sorry if I caused any problems."

Scott assured me no harm was done. "Your timing couldn't have been any better." Then he explained they had just come home a few minutes before I arrived, and he was actually trying to think of a nice way to end the relationship.

We sat on the beanbag chairs and talked for hours about things that had taken place in our lives during the last three months. For the first time in years, we just openly talked with no pressure or judgment toward each other. We enjoyed each other's company, and I saw him in a new light. We were falling in love all over again.

I spent the next few nights at Michele's house while Scott and I worked things out. The timing was perfect, and we were being given a second chance.

While I stayed with Michele, she was working on some poetry. I asked if she would teach me. This is what I wrote:

TO THE ONE I LOVE

Sometimes when I think of you,
It's all I can do.

Sometimes when I think of why,
The answers will arrive.

And then, I find myself driving all night,
Just to find my great knight.

And when I find this great love of my life,
Everything suddenly seems so right.

So I quit asking why this love seems so right;
For when I look at your heart, the future seems so bright.

It's not hard to learn how love and energy flow;
All you have to do is believe, and you'll know.
As free as the wind, are you and I,
and oh, how our spirits do soar;

But together, my love, we can do so much more.

Chapter 28

Tormented Souls

SCOTT ALREADY HAD SIGNED a six-month lease on a two-bedroom apartment in the city, as he could no longer afford to rent our house in the country. The small apartment was located in a sketchy part of Minneapolis, but it was cheap. The apartment buildings formed a U that faced a busy, elevated interstate, and the noise bounced from one building to the next. I found the contrast startling after the months I had just spent in the wilderness.

The living room window faced the parking lot, where many people played loud music while working on their cars. Outside our bedroom window stretched a steelyard, where the beeping of large trucks followed by huge crashing sounds woke us early every morning. If that weren't enough, the Minneapolis-St. Paul International Airport was just a few miles away, and the flight pattern went right over us. The noise was deafening, and the vibration shook the windows, dishes, and cupboards. I had to plug my ears every ten minutes during peak landing times to block the painful sound while the planes flew over.

Train tracks ran on the other side of the parking lot. The trains blew a loud, foghorn whistle as they passed, but it didn't bother me. The sound was the only one I found comforting, because it reminded me of the good times when I had stayed at my grandma's house as a child.

The new apartment shocked my nervous system. I had spent three months in the wilderness, and now I found myself in the middle of a busy, noisy city. In the wilderness, I became sensitized to my surroundings, and my physical senses increased in awareness. In the city, I heard every little noise and saw all kinds of movements. My senses constantly were overloaded.

I had no choice but to desensitize. I hated losing the spiritual ground I had gained, but I had to close down my world to tunnel vision, or I would have gone completely mad.

It took about a month to lose the sensitivity I had gained. I noticed that, as my awareness and peacefulness slowly began to slip away, they were replaced by stress and the fast pace of the city. A part of my well-being started to die. I was losing the connection to my life source. Too many things happened around me at once, and I couldn't process it all and remain calm and peaceful.

I decided to research indigenous cultures to help ease my stress, and I found a Native American shop down the road that sold art and crafts. They also offered classes on making some of the items. I couldn't resist, and that's when I met Tismal.

Tismal, a soft-spoken Native American, worked at the shop. He was a kind man who was slow to meet a person's eyes. Skilled in beadwork, leatherwork, quillwork, and numerous other crafts, he was also knowledgeable in herbs and medicinal plant usage. He was a great find, or so I thought.

I love being creative, and I wanted to find someone willing to teach me more skills. At first, I just took a few basic classes offered at the little shop. It soon became apparent to Tismal that I wanted to learn more than what was offered. That's when he agreed to teach me, along with a few others, in private classes.

We learned about the history of the materials we were using to make many of the items. Not only did we learn how to do beadwork, but we spent hours discovering where the beads came from and how to identify them and their cultural significance. We also learned how to use quills, leather, bark, and feathers. We used these items to create bags, pouches, gloves, and moccasins covered with intricate bead or quillwork.

Tismal told us the stories behind each item as we worked, explaining their purpose and design. I studied with him during the winter months, which was great, considering the cold, harsh Minnesota winters cause a lot of people to struggle with cabin fever, myself included. He was good at explaining the spiritual purpose behind each item, and he possessed amazing healing gifts. One day, he mixed some herbs and placed them in a line down my back.

That night, I felt incredible peace and dropped into a deep state of awareness. All my aches and pains were gone, and I slept well for the first time since moving to the city.

Tismal could also hold an item that belonged to someone and tell you about that person's life. I was able to do the same thing, but I didn't understand how it worked. I was hoping Tismal could shed some light on where this ability came from. He was the first person who could read me. But he didn't know anything more than I did about why we could do these things. I wouldn't learn until much later that, even though we had this amazing gift given to us by Creator, we still lacked something very important.

At the time, I was trying to connect what Native Americans believed and my experiences. Like putting together a giant jigsaw puzzle, some pieces fit while others did not. I became obsessed with discovering my purpose in life. I had searched everywhere for someone to teach me more about spirituality. I wasn't sure where else to look, so I stayed with the Native American theme and followed up on every lead.

After meeting Tismal, I ran errands and drove him to his destinations in exchange for teaching me. I even went as far as letting him come live with us. At first, Scott was annoyed, but then he became intrigued. Tismal was a great artist and made all kinds of things. The arrangement was like having a personal teacher. I picked up a few nuggets of information I wasn't taught in the wilderness classes, but spiritually, I felt deflated. Even the inner voice I often heard seemed silent, because of the constant barrage of noise and interruptions.

Observing people was one of my favorite things to do. With plenty of people around me, I focused on that, but my drive to find new teachers led me into some pretty wild places. One night, Tismal, who was staying with us at the time, took me to a nightclub to meet a woman who supposedly knew a lot about medicinal plants and their spiritual meanings.

I had never been to a nightclub before. When we went inside, I saw girls dancing with girls and guys with guys. I knew little about this world.

We were barely inside the door when Tismal said, "Wait here. I'll be right back."

Right back from where? I sat at the first available table.

A waiter asked if I would like anything to drink.

"Water will be fine."

I observed the couples around me in this room that featured a small dance floor. The nightclub was made up of several rooms, including an upper level, but I wasn't about to move beyond my spot for the moment. I carefully watched each person on the dance floor. The amount of alcohol consumed seemed excessive.

"Why?" I whispered to myself. *Why do people feel they have to get drunk to have a good time?*

While I sipped my water, a group of women approached, asking if I would like to dance.

"No," I said. "I'm just waiting for a friend to return."

As they were leaving, I glanced at the clock on the wall. Twenty minutes had gone by, and still no sign of Tismal. I grew antsy, having been left alone in a world I knew little about.

Finally, after more time passed, it became apparent I would have to get up and search for Tismal. I considered just leaving him there, but we were in a not-so-safe part of downtown, and I would have to walk through an unfamiliar alley to return to the car.

As I was making my way to the second room, I suddenly felt as if I was in a bubble—like I stood in a glass sphere. "Souls," I whispered. "I see souls."

Waves of colored light started to sway from the people as they danced. I blinked my eyes and shook my head, thinking it was some kind of illusion. Yet, I could see them clear as day. Auras surrounded them, like the ones I had seen in the wilderness classes, but there was a difference. It reminded me of the day I was returning home from the hospital after my near-death experience when I had stared out the car window, and the wheat seemed to be waving at me in slow motion. Every hue and tone surpassed anything I had ever seen.

The swaying light here in the nightclub was the same and, as I watched the auras swaying across the room, everything went into slow motion. I just stood there, amazed. I knew the light surrounding each person was their spirit, but I also could see deep into their souls.

Still encased in my bubble, I walked through the crowd. I could see a core being in each person searching for some sense of identity. Some were being tormented, and I could see their pain. Their souls were weeping.

I wanted to help, but I didn't know how. When I reached the other side of the room, the auras faded. I could no longer see into their souls. The bubble, or sphere, I was in also disappeared, and the dancing speed returned to normal. I stepped inside another room and found people in all kinds of costumes and masks. Every identity was shielded, making it impossible to tell anything about any one person.

I kept moving until I found Tismal sitting near the end of a long bar. "What are you doing?"

"Suuuue," Tismal slurred, already clearly drunk. "I was just coming to get you."

Sure. I knew full well he had merely used me to get to this bar. The woman he promised to introduce me to probably didn't even exist.

I realized then that I had been naïve. I wasn't a city girl, so I didn't know the ways or the language of the city. This was not where I would discover any of the answers to my spiritual questions. I had wanted so badly to learn more about the spirit realm that all my common sense had left.

The next morning, I told Tismal he had one week to move out.

Chapter 29

Spiritual Awareness

AFTER TISMAL MOVED OUT, Scott and I made plans to move back to Colorado. Even though I was eager to return to Colorado, the act of getting there was another question. We had no money, no jobs to go to, and no place to live. Yet, we had started over from scratch before, so we should be able to do it again.

Scott wasn't against the idea. After all, we loved Colorado, and he would be away from his Minneapolis friends who did drugs. He just didn't see how we could survive financially, and frankly, neither did I.

Four weeks later, the decision was pretty much made for us. When Scott returned home from work, he took my hands and said, "You're not going to believe this, Sue. I lost my job."

"What?"

"The company is closing." He pulled back and smiled. "We might as well make a fresh start in Colorado."

"Yes!" I shouted.

We immediately began making plans. By the time we paid for the U-Haul truck and set aside enough gas money to reach Colorado, we only had eight hundred dollars. We decided that was enough. On January first, 1995, we left Minnesota and headed for Colorado.

We stayed with Scott's sister, Sandy, in Fort Collins for a few days while we searched for work and a place to live. We liked the town of Boulder and decided to move there. Scott found work right away, and I found a gallery that rented me space to sell my artwork. My Native American pieces, especially the dream catchers, were a big hit. We also connected with some classmates from the wilderness survival school who lived in the area.

It felt good to be back in Colorado. Things were definitely on an upward swing. Scott and I were finding healing in our relationship, and we had friends to practice our survival skills with. I even completed my bachelor's degree in wilderness education at Prescott College.

That spring, we received a special invitation to a course offered by Dave's survival and awareness school. Attendance was by invitation only, and they didn't charge for the class. The things we ended up doing in this class were so risky, we had to sign a waiver saying we were just a bunch of friends getting together for a week of camping. If we died or were seriously hurt, it was no one's fault but our own.

Scott and I were excited and nervous about this class, which demanded top-notch physical and spiritual skills to survive. Fifteen people were chosen out of a few hundred qualified students—three women and twelve men. No meals were provided, so everyone brought their own food and supplies for the week.

The first day was intimidating. I knew one of the women and a few of the men. Several men from Canada and the United States had military backgrounds. Scott thought it was really cool to connect and be a part of an elite group. I soon realized physical strength wasn't the only quality needed to succeed in this course.

We were each dropped off a few miles from camp for our first exercise. The hour was late, and the moon wasn't out yet. The only rule was to keep our blindfolds on. We were to find our way back to camp blindfolded. We had all night to complete the challenge. Victory would come if we made it back before sunrise. I had come to like these challenges, but this one was going to push my limits.

I stood in the woods breathing in the smell of pine trees and trying to decide the best way to approach this exercise.

I tied my blindfold on and took several deep breaths. Every forest sound was immediately amplified. Something to the right made a crackling sound. Was it a coyote or was it a mouse? A snap to the left brought my head around. Was it one of the wild dogs? Or a PACK of dogs? Panic hit me.

Oh my gosh, I'm really alone.

I was tempted to pull off the blindfold. Instead, I calmed myself and began to put one foot in front of the other. I had no idea where I was or even if I was going in the correct direction. I tried to shove panic down by encouraging myself. *You have done this before. You can do it again.*

I inched forward, trusting my inner vision to guide me. My feet found spots unhampered by running vines. Nothing jumped out of the night to grab me. Soon, I was back in rhythm. I sensed approaching tree branches that I needed to duck under or go around. After several hours of walking, I still didn't know if I was moving in the right direction. I sat down to rest and removed the blindfold to see where I was.

In the dim moonlight, everything looked the same. I was seated in a small clearing surrounded by pine trees. I heard no human voices and had no idea which direction camp was located. Nothing looked familiar. I was lost. Panic started to set in again. I wondered how anyone would ever find me, even in the daylight.

I kept the blindfold off and picked a direction I thought seemed right. Then I began to walk, hoping to come across an area I recognized.

Things quickly grew worse.

The smooth path disappeared, and I began to trip over branches until I was completely caught up in underbrush. I pulled myself up and thrashed through the woods, becoming even more panicked. Finally, I stopped and listened.

Nothing.

"Is anyone out there?" I called.

Nothing.

"Is anyone close to me?"

Still nothing.

"Can anybody hear me?" I yelled.

No one yelled back.

I managed to hold back fear, but just barely. I calmed myself with encouraging self-talk. "You can do this," I told myself again, "You've done it before."

I thought about my situation. My first thought was to keep walking without the blindfold and call for help every few minutes. My next thought was just to sit there until someone came looking for me. Neither choice seemed right, so I decided to try prayer.

I was desperate.

I believed Creator God existed, but I didn't know if He really cared about me. I decided to test Him out. "God," I said, "please help me. I'm lost." It wasn't a fancy or long prayer. It was simple, sincere, and right to the point.

Within seconds I heard very clearly in my mind, *"Put your blindfold back on."*

"What?" I glanced around, surprised.

"Put the blindfold back on," the Voice said again.

Even though I had prayed, I hadn't truly expected to hear such a clear and quick answer. Because the response was so direct, I did what the Voice said. I put the blindfold back on and sat there.

"Now get up and start walking."

I walked. I was in no position to argue with God.

I no longer tripped or struggled through the brush as I moved forward. God was guiding me, and the walk was effortless. With each step, I felt more and more confident. A higher power was leading me. This was the Creator I had been trusting all along.

I walked about thirty more minutes with the blindfold on. By this time, I was walking at a pretty good clip. Then I tripped over a berm of dirt and fell to my hands and knees. The landing was soft, because I had fallen in a sandy area, so I started crawling. I could explore the ground better on my hands and knees. After several minutes, I realized I had stumbled onto a small sandy road. Was it possible? Was this the road back to camp?

I stood and listened. The faint crunching of debris sounded to my right.

"Who's there?" I called.

"It's me, Bill."

Relief flooded me. It was so good to know I wasn't alone. Not only that, but I was also pretty sure this was the road back to camp. Victory was close. "Do you still have your blindfold on?" I asked.

"Yes. How about you?"

"It's still on," I said. "I think we are on the road that leads back to camp."

"I think you're right. But which way do we go?"

I took a minute to think about it. If we went the wrong way, we would probably never make it back to camp in time. "I feel drawn to move toward the right."

"Okay," he said. "I'll go that way too."

Within five minutes, we were both back in camp. When we took our blindfolds off, the sky was beginning to lighten in the east. We had made it back before sunrise. We jumped up and down, whooping in victory. "We did it!" we yelled. I'm sure our voices echoed throughout the entire forest.

I don't believe I would have found my way back to camp if I hadn't put the blindfold back on and trusted God to lead. I have since discovered that's how it is in life. When I worry and fret over life's challenges, panic often sets in. When I trust God, things go much better, and I experience peace and victory. God, my Creator, cares about me.

Chapter 30

Night Games

SCOTT ARRIVED IN CAMP about thirty minutes later, just before sunrise. We both celebrated. After the adrenaline wore off, exhaustion took over. We staggered back to our tent, where we collapsed into a deep sleep.

At breakfast, Scott and I talked about what we experienced during the blindfold exercise.

"I felt the presence of large masses in front of me like trees," Scott said. "At one point, I got stabbed by a thorn in my arm. I took two steps back and moved sideways."

"What happened next?"

"I got the urge to get down on my hands and knees and started crawling."

"Did you get all caught up in the briers?"

"Actually," Scott said, "I found myself crawling through some kind of small animal run. I didn't have to go very far before I stood up again."

"How did you know when to stand up?"

"Something inside told me it was time." He looked up from his plate. "I took my blindfold off to get my bearings. I could smell campfire smoke drifting through the pines and recognized I was on the northern perimeter of camp. I put my blindfold back on and walked toward the smell of smoke."

"That's amazing," I said. "I had a similar experience. Several hours into the walk, I felt lost and alone, so I prayed to God for help."

"I believe God is in all of this," Scott said. "He's part of every religion and New Age spirituality."

Something about what Scott said didn't feel right. My paradigm was beginning to shift. I had seen and experienced too much to believe Scott's theory was true anymore, but I didn't have time to think about it, because Ben's voice boomed, "Come on, everyone! We have to go find all those who didn't make it back to camp last night."

Scott stood. "This will be fun. We are going to look great, because we made it back."

I laughed. I was thinking more about the poor lost people and was hoping they were okay. Looking great was not a priority for me, but I understood Scott's frustration at being known as Sue's husband. Most people didn't know we were divorced, because we were living together. Scott wanted to be known for his own achievements.

"Let's go!" Ben yelled.

We searched for more than two hours and finally found the students we sought. They were all miles away, meandering on different two-track roads that ran through the Pine Barrens. They simply found a road and planted themselves until help came. All the missing students were fine except for hurt pride.

Once everyone was safely back at camp, we spent the days working on advanced traps and tracking. We had to do this during the day, because the traps were so deadly. We didn't want anyone killed. After we built the traps, we immediately took them apart. I never realized how dangerous and evil things could get. Dave had told us many people hole up away from civilization and set traps like this, not caring if they caught a human in them.

In the afternoons, we worked on man tracking. Some of the military guys told us stories about how you have to be careful when you track criminals, because they can circle around and track you. They talked about a Canadian officer who lost his life in a scenario similar to the lesson they were describing. It sent chills up my spine. This was serious business. Same with the traps. At that moment, I no longer wanted to be involved.

I felt an anxiety attack coming on. I needed to get centered again, so I went to my favorite spot in the cedar swamp. I sat on the stump and began to relax. I closed my eyes, breathed in the scent of cedar and vegetation, and listened to birdsong and falling water slowly moving through the cedars. This was the world where I belonged.

When I opened my eyes, I had lost track of time. It had to be late afternoon or early evening because the sun rode low in the sky.

Scott would be hungry and eager to prepare dinner, so I walked out and sat on a knoll facing the cedar swamp. That's when I noticed the auras.

Several students knew I could see auras, especially at this time of day. Several came down and joined me on the knoll.

"Will you teach us how to see auras?" Ben asked.

"Sure," I said. "Look over at the cedar swamp but stay in wide-angle vision."

"I don't see anything," Ben said as three others joined in.

I pointed upward. "Stare at the treetops, but not directly. Look at them through your peripheral vision."

It wasn't long before Sarah shouted, "I see them!"

"Me too!" chimed in Ben.

We all high-fived each other and then headed for dinner.

After we ate, Ben prepped us for that night's game. We were sectioned into three groups. After dark, each group would form a circle around a flag using a single lantern as the only light. Some would stay back and defend their camp, while others would try and sneak into the other camps. We used all the tools available to us, both physical and spiritual, to detect the enemy before they penetrated our camp. The team who captured the flag without being detected would be the winners. It was kind of like Capture-the-flag on steroids.

I was in the first group that formed a circle with the lantern and flag in the center. As I sat at my post inside the circle staring into the woods, I started thinking about auras. Could I see them at night? Not just the trails they left behind like with the animals when we spirit tracked, but could I see them coming toward me in the present?

I closed my eyes and looked into the forest with my spiritual eyes. Sure enough, I saw a group jogging in a straight line down a dirt trail toward us. The leader's aura was bright red, and I tasted cinnamon every time I looked at him. I watched him move through the woods and hide behind trees until he was within calling distance.

"Kevin!" I yelled. "I see you hiding behind the bush next to the tall pine tree."

"What?" he called. "How did you know it was me? You can't even see this far. And it's dark!"

"I saw you guys jogging up the road, and you tasted like cinnamon."

"What!" He couldn't believe what he was hearing.

When we returned to camp, everyone wanted to know how I could see them. The problem was, I didn't know. I hadn't really tried to do anything. All I did was close my eyes and believe it was possible. But the other students were so eager to learn that I told them I would try to teach them the next morning.

After crawling into my sleeping bag, I thought about the events that took place earlier that evening. I whispered as I fell asleep, "God, if you're in any of this, please let me know."

Chapter 31

The Haunted House

THE NEXT MORNING everyone was excited to discover my secret. I still didn't know what my secret was, but I was willing to share whatever I could. After breakfast, I took a few students who couldn't see auras down to the cedar swamp.

I stood in front of them with my back to the cedars. "Look at me through your peripheral vision. What color is my aura?"

"Light blue," some said.

I closed my eyes and focused on a certain color. "Now, what color do you see?"

"Purple."

"Good," I said.

I felt excited that they actually saw the color change, or at least two of them could. "Now, I'm going to stack another color on top of the purple. Can you see it?"

"I see a golden color," Sarah said.

"I see it too!" Ben shouted.

I smiled. "Good job! I'm now going to add a taste." I closed my eyes again and imagined the taste of salt. "What do you taste?"

"Salt," said Kevin. "I couldn't see anything, but I can taste salt."

"Great," I said.

"How did you do that?" The other students wanted to know.

I shrugged. "I just use my imagination and willpower to make it manifest."

That's amazing," Kevin said. "But how do you see colors at night?"

"I'm not sure. I just do. Maybe if you practice, it will happen for you too."

I tried to give encouragement, but I suspected practicing might not work for everyone. I told them how I had simply focused on seeing auras. I started out looking at an object, not straight on, but through my peripheral vision, then being patient until I could actually see a color. Once I could see the color, an amazing thing happened. It would expand and, if the wind were blowing through the trees, it would create trails of colors. I had my own light show, similar to the northern lights.

While the others continued to practice, I went off by myself. I sat in the cedar swamp for what seemed like hours.

Hopefully, I would gain some insight into why I could see auras better than most people.

Nothing made sense. Why could I see auras at night so clearly? Why was I able to change the color of my aura? And what was the taste all about?

I decided to talk to God. I told him how much I appreciated all He had done for me the other night when I was lost in the woods. "But I have more questions than answers at the moment," I told Him. "Will you please show me how all this stuff I'm doing fits together?"

I didn't receive my answer then but, years later, I learned I had been seeing through my spiritual eyes. I was seeing an energy field that emanated from a living being. The spiritual realm doesn't operate with the same laws as the physical realm. That's why I could see auras at night. The energy field comes from the spirit.

Yet, while I sat there in the cedar swamp, I still didn't have any answers. I didn't hear any voice from God. In fact, all I could hear was Ben yelling.

"It's time for debriefing!"

Ben's yell jolted me back to the military style so common with some of the men. We had reached our last morning, and, for once, I was glad to be done. I knew in my spirit that my time here at this particular school was finished. After nearly a decade of classes, I wouldn't be back. The classes had started to feel repetitive, and I believed there was more to be learned than Dave could teach. It was time to graduate to something more.

But what is that something more?

I thought back through all the classes I had taken and about my search for what happens when we die. I had experienced both light and dark in the spiritual realm, but I still didn't know how to live consistently in the light. I also had experienced a personal connection with God. Was such an experience a passing thing? Or was that connection something a person could experience on a regular basis?

I didn't know, but I was determined to find out. So, after our debriefing, Scott and I said our goodbyes to the others and left.

We took several days to recover once we arrived home. We were beyond exhaustion. Then our landlord informed us we had to find a new place. We wanted to live in a house up in the mountains, but they were too expensive.

I decided to talk with my friend, Robin, who led a primitive skills school called Earth Knack. Robin connected me with Denise. I recognized her from previous primitive skills gatherings, but I never got to know her personally. She and her boyfriend, Mike, also were looking for a house in the mountains. Like Scott and me, they couldn't afford one.

"Why don't you two get a place together?" Robin suggested.

Denise's eyes widened. "What a great idea." Then she turned to me. "I've found the perfect place already. It's in the mountains and has plenty of room for all of us."

"Sweet," I said. "Let's do it."

What a relief to have all the worry fall away and have a plan in mind. I hardly cared what the place looked like. I just wanted to be in the mountains. We were young and could handle any challenge. But I had not thought about the challenge of moving into a haunted house. Of course, we did not know that piece of information in the beginning.

Denise and I both talked with our partners, and they readily agreed. Scott and Mike met for the first time at the rental with the landlord already there. We had to pretend we had been friends forever. We even gave each other hugs.

It worked. She believed we were old friends, and we rented the house.

I loved making new friends and being back in the woods again.

The house, old and dark, had a life of its own. Strange things began happening. The first occurred in the dimly lit cinder block room we all had to go through to reach the stairs leading into the house. A wicker chair hung from the ceiling, and a tiny window sat up high in the wall.

Every time I crossed through the room, I experienced an eerie feeling. The sensation became creepier each time until finally, one day, I caught a glimpse of a woman out of the corner of my eye.

Oh my God, there is a woman sitting in the wicker chair. Her head was frozen in place, and she was staring out the window.

I sped up the stairs.

After that, I saw the woman every time I went through the room. She had a single gray braid and sat as still as a statue. She wasn't translucent or glowing, and her skin was ashen. I eventually grew used to her being there, but the creepy feeling never left.

One day, Denise and I ate lunch together, and we discovered we had both seen the old lady. The sightings freaked her out as much as they did me. Neither of us had any answers other than the house must be haunted.

One time, when everyone had to work late, I was home alone making dream catchers on the third level of the house. I started hearing noises in the rooms below, doors opening and shutting, and the creaking of floorboards.

"Who's there?" I called, thinking one of my roommates was returning home.

No one answered.

I moved to the top of the stairs and called again. "Who's there?"

A door slammed below.

No way was I going down there to check it out. Cell phones didn't work in our remote cabin, and I had no way of communicating with anyone. Terrified, I went back to my room, sat on my bed, and prayed for someone to come home.

After that, if I knew everyone was coming home late, I drove an hour to town and waited. I didn't tell anyone what was going on, because it was too weird. I figured things would change soon when the days grew longer. But that's when the nightmares started happening, and the walls in the room began to whisper.

Of course, the walls didn't really whisper, but I kept hearing murmuring and began seeing dark shadows flying around the room. These incidences reminded me of the dark things I had seen while attending Dave's courses. I had no idea why I would see those kinds of things here in Colorado, but I never stayed alone after dark in that house again.

At this time, I began to see a connection between the physical and spiritual realm. I knew I was a part of both worlds. They were connected, and one world could not exist without the other. But how could I operate in both at the same time?

Even though years had passed since my near-death experience, I was still determined to find answers. Key pieces of the puzzle were still missing.

Meanwhile, Denise and Mike had joined a business organization called Amway. They asked if they could give us a presentation. "We just want to see if we are doing it right," Denise said.

They gave us such a great presentation that we decided to join. We started attending meetings and training on how to present the business opportunity to others. We had no idea at the time how important this opportunity would be in leading us to the light.

Yet, at the time, the light seemed far away. The shadows and nightmares were growing worse. My cat slept at the top of my head, staying as close as possible. I often woke with him hissing at the shadows flying around the room as if he was trying to protect me. After four months in the haunted house, I made an excuse about the high elevation bothering me. I rented a room from my old landlady so that I could sleep at night. While there, I began to look for another place for Scott and me.

A war was going on for my soul, and I didn't even know it.

Chapter 32

Warnings

I STILL SPENT TIME AT THE HAUNTED HOUSE during the day, as long as someone else was home. All my supplies for making dream catchers and my personal belongings were still there. One day, Denise and I talked about close calls we had both experienced and how, we probably wouldn't be alive if we hadn't listened to that voice of warning.

She told me a story that had recently happened on a day when it had begun to snow. She was exhausted and driving home from work, looking for the quickest way possible, when she heard a Voice say, "Go get some oil for your car."

Oh yeah, I have to remember to pick up some oil. She continued on her way, certain she had enough oil to make it home. She would get oil tomorrow.

"Get some oil now!" the Voice said, louder.

Denise was used to hearing voices from the spiritual realm, so she argued with the Voice. She pulled up to an intersection, but when she moved forward, her car suddenly turned right and headed toward a small town. Frustrated about driving in a direction that took her farther from home, she said aloud, “Fine. I’ll go get the oil.”

She arrived at the store but couldn’t find any oil, so she headed back the way she had come. By now, she was beyond exhaustion, and the snow was coming down harder. She passed the intersection where she had originally turned off her route, berating herself for listening to the silly voice.

The pavement became a sheet of ice a few miles down the road. Before long, she spotted a fleet of flashing lights ahead. As she approached the twisted mass of cars, tears began to well. Likely, no one had survived. If she had not listened to the Voice and stopped for the oil, she might have been part of that horrifying accident.

She shook and trembled the rest of the way home. She knew God had saved her life that night.

“How do you know it was God who saved you?” I asked.

“Who else would it be? The devil sure doesn’t want me to live,” Denise said.

“Is God the only one who helps you?”

“Sometimes angels do,” she said, “but God sends them. So, yes, He’s the only one.”

I decided to tell her about a similar situation my friend Michelle had. She had been driving on a four-lane highway when a tunnel loomed ahead. Each direction had two lanes going through the dark tunnel. Michelle was driving the speed limit and came upon a car moving considerably slower. She decided to pass, but when she began to move into the left lane, she heard a voice say, "No! Don't pass!"

Startled, she slowed and returned to her lane. After looking around and realizing no one in the car had spoken to her, she once again tried to move into the passing lane.

As she pulled out, the voice spoke again. "No!" it insisted. "Get back into the other lane."

This time, she recognized the voice as an ancestor, and a face also appeared before her. She immediately swerved the car back into her lane and screamed as a car roared by, going the wrong way. The oncoming car's headlights were off, and the driver probably didn't even know he was going in the wrong direction.

"Michelle only hears this ancestor's voice when she is in danger," I said to Denise. "That's how God communicates with her about dangerous situations."

"Wow!" Denise said. "It's good to know I'm not the only one."

"You're not," I assured her. "In fact, it reminds me of a time when I was twelve years old." I recounted the story of walking a secluded country road to deliver a candle to our neighbor's house. The house sat about a mile away, and no other neighbors lived between us. Halfway there, an old black car slowly passed then stopped in front of me.

I remember smelling the burning oil of the exhaust, and I tensed. Something wasn't right.

The man stepped out of his car and walked toward me. He was dressed in black, with black hair and black-framed glasses.

I was about to take off running when a voice said, *"Don't move!"*

I stood frozen with the candle clenched in my fist, ready to throw at the man.

He had left his car door open and stopped four feet in front of me.

I stared at his mouth, because I never looked anyone in the eyes back then. His lips were pale.

"Do you want a ride?" he asked.

"No," I said.

The man shifted from one foot to the other, then he looked up at the sky and back down at me. Several times, he looked down the street both ways as if to see if anyone was coming. "Are you sure you don't need a ride someplace?"

"No. I'm fine."

He stood there a long time, staring at me with a puzzled look. Then his expression and body posture started to change. An internal struggle was happening, so I remained motionless and watched him. I was in trouble, but the voice continued to tell me to remain still.

Finally, the man began shaking his head, turned around, and walked back to his car.

"Run now!" the voice said.

I didn't have to be told twice. I bolted toward a thicket of trees and briars that formed a fencerow separating each field. The snow had drifted deep in spots, but that didn't slow me. When I reached the fencerow, I hid beneath a thicket of briars and trees, not daring to look up. As I hunched there, motionless, I heard the man's car pass by several times. Finally, when the coast was clear, I walked home using the fields and tree lines as cover.

"Do you think that was God speaking to me?" I asked Denise.

"Absolutely," she said. "You're going to love Rick and Mona, who are our sponsors in Amway. They will be able to tell you more about God and Jesus."

"Why? Did they have an experience like this also?"

"I don't know, but they are the first Christians I've met who walk the talk."

"What do you mean?"

"They lead by example and show how strong a relationship can be when you both walk with God. You're going to love them."

I raised my eyebrows and looked at Denise. "That will be a first."

Chapter 33

Nor'easter

Boulder, Colorado, 1998

SCOTT AND I FOUND A PLACE for rent in Boulder and moved out of the haunted house. Once we were settled, we could build our Amway business. Rick and Mona plugged us into their personal growth development program. We read one book a month and listened to a few tapes a week.

Although I wasn't thrilled with Amway as a business, I loved learning and growing into the person I wanted to become, a businesswoman who did things in the outdoors. I dreamed of leading primitive technology classes. Becoming financially independent would allow me to do what I really wanted.

We were told a three-day business convention in Maine was important for our business and personal growth. We should be there, so we went. The last day of the convention fell on Sunday morning, and two thousand people gathered in the auditorium. The speaker was a preacher, which I found odd. I was tired from the previous two days, and I found it hard to focus while he spoke.

I wasn't paying attention at the end when he gave us some kind of invitation to come forward. People around me rose and walked to the stage. They wept and hugged each other. I had no idea what was going on. Embarrassed, I sank into my chair. *This is a business convention. Why are these people going forward and weeping?* They seemed weak.

Then, I felt drawn to go myself, but I wasn't sure why. So, I fought the urge. Scott was still sitting next to me. I didn't want to look like a fool.

The chairs emptied as most of the people went forward. Then, the preacher had them repeat some words. It seemed as if they had all gone crazy. When the meeting ended, many people were still weeping. Others began to file out for lunch. I sat there a few minutes, trying to gather my composure and process what had just happened. I couldn't get my mind around it. After the room emptied, Scott and I walked out to the lobby.

Rick and Mona greeted us. I liked this couple. They modeled what I believed following Jesus should look like, just like Denise said they would. They didn't just talk about how to live a life of integrity, they lived it. They were always complementing and encouraging each other and were willing to help others in any way they could.

I wanted to live that kind of integrity. I thought about asking them how they did it, but I never got a chance. As we made our way across the crowd, all my spiritual thoughts fell behind, replaced with business and busyness. Our schedules kicked in, and we were back on a timeline.

Later, while driving home, I began to think about the spiritual once again. Why did all those people go forward to the stage?

It seemed I had missed out on something important. I still had no idea what had happened, but something was drawing me, and the pull was nearly as strong as the bright light in my near-death experience. I could hardly wait for the next convention, half a year away in January. I would go forward with all those other people, even though I had no idea what it was all about. I wanted to connect spiritually like they did.

Six months later, at the next Amway convention, every ounce of my being was drawn to Sunday morning. I no longer cared about the business stuff. I couldn't wait to go forward to that stage. But when I woke Sunday morning, a nor'easter howled in full force with the snow blowing sideways.

January is one of the worst times to drive the I-80 corridor along the Great Lakes. Not only are arctic blasts common, but lake-effect snow is usually inevitable, which means the roads may soon be treacherous. Even if the Interstate remained open, I would struggle to drive the thirty-five hours by myself nonstop in such a storm. In two hours, I would have to drive home alone while Scott took a plane. I stared out the window of the hotel, but I could see nothing but blowing snow.

I had heard that God answers the prayers of new Christians more than others. I wasn't a Christian yet, but I figured now might be a good time to make a deal.

"God, if you're real," I prayed. "I need the weather to be good and the roads clear all the way home." I knew, as I watched the snow piling high, if He answered that prayer, then He was real.

Scott and I headed for the Sunday morning service. I heard little of the message, but as soon as the preacher gave the invitation to come forward, I was the first to run to the stage. Emotions I didn't understand overwhelmed me. I stared at the floor. If I looked up, I would weep. Still, I couldn't keep the tears back. I had no idea why.

The next few minutes were a blur as the preacher asked us to repeat his words. I asked Jesus to be my Lord and Savior and come into my heart. I don't know where the change came from, my thinking of Creator to God to Jesus, but the connection was very real. I somehow knew they were all one.

Scott stood beside me. I don't know when he appeared, but I was grateful we were on the same page. Many people around us were crying. The people in the back of the crowd sobbed the loudest. I could feel the presence of God in my entire being. Though not quite as powerful as my near-death experience, this moment was recognizable as coming from the same source.

At the end of the service, the preacher said it was really important to find a Bible-based church to get involved in. He also said that God would lead us to the right place when we returned home.

I never realized people like this pastor existed. He didn't want anything from me, and he was genuinely kind to everyone. I knew in my heart that he worshiped the same God who had been leading me. He was definitely in touch with the spiritual realm, a part of the Christian world I had never seen before, and it gave me hope.

When Scott and I walked out those conference doors, not a cloud etched the sky. The sun sparkled off the snow, and the pavement was clear.

Scott squeezed my hand. The nor'easter had blown itself out.

"God," I whispered, "you heard me."

Chapter 34

Looking Back

I HAD LOTS OF TIME TO THINK during my long drive home on roads clear of ice and snow the entire way. I finally had discovered that the Creator who spoke me into existence also cared intimately about me.

I could look back over my life and see His tracks so clearly. He was the old Indian man who appeared in my visions and dreams. He was the Voice who warned me as a child and saved me from the man who meant me harm. He was the Wind who rocked me in our maple tree. He was the Protector who pulled me from the nightmares in my visions of hell. He was the Presence who filled me with peace the night of the sweat lodge when I lay beneath the moon. He was the Light who drew me when I had my near-death experience. He was all those yet so much more.

He is pure love. Without Him, I would not exist. He taught me how to open my spiritual eyes and see into a realm that's more real than the physical.

I believe God talks to everybody and often warns us of upcoming danger, but we get caught up in the daily busyness of life, and we don't stay in tune with His voice. The Voice becomes muddled in with all the other stress of life. I am amazed God never gave up on me. He used the years spent in all the survival and awareness classes to teach and reach me. He walked the paths I already was walking.

I finally knew where I was going when I died. I chose the Light. I now knew that the one true God, who is love, is the one true Light of the world, and His name is Jesus. I had made the choice where I would spend eternity. The answer had found me. The answer had been there all along, but it took years for me to finally understand.

Chapter 35

The Answer

I HAVE EXPERIENCED A LOT OF DARK places on my journey to discover what happens when we die. I was fortunate to make it through alive, but some are not so fortunate. One of my classmates died because of believing in the wrong kind of healing. Another classmate committed suicide because of all the dark voices in his head. The dark side is a dangerous place, affecting every part of our being.

The good news is the Light also affects every part of our being. I've been to hell and back, but I've also been to the Light and back. The Light filled me with peace, something the darkness never gave me.

I used to feel as if I carried this huge weight on my shoulders, but now it is gone. My life changed when I chose Jesus.

Walking with God is powerful. I have experienced, and am still experiencing, many miracles of healing and restoration. I'm truly free to be who I was created to be. Before, I was trying to be something I wasn't, but now I'm connected to the One who created everything. My life has meaning and a deeper purpose.

I had a choice to make while I was still alive on Earth. Where was I going to spend eternity?

Each of us has a choice. We don't just disappear after we die. The decision about where we will spend eternity must be made before we physically die here on Earth. I made my decision when I accepted Jesus as my Savior. I know where I'm going to spend eternity. After all, it's only forever.

And if that isn't blessing enough, I also have Scott to go through it all with me, because he has changed as well, and our relationship is stronger than ever.

On April 2, 2002, Scott and I traveled up to Rocky National Park and found a beautiful little spot on the river. Rain poured from the sky. But for a few moments, while we said our wedding vows to each other, the sky opened up above us. A beam of sunlight hit the river. There were no other people. We basked in the sunlight and watched it sparkle on the water, then it started to rain, and we ran for the car. But just for a moment, the heavens shined upon us.

God hears the cry of every heart.

ABOUT

Sue Halvorsen lives a life filled with adventure. She loves the outdoors and is an avid supporter of animal rescue, both wild and domestic. She earned a Bachelors' degree in Wilderness education and traveled to many wild places. Yet, the most amazing place she has visited is the edge of eternity.

CONTACT

To learn more about Sue and receive a free gift visit:

thewindsofhope.com

Free Audio Gift

@

thewindsofhope.com

How To Hear From God